THE FRANK W. PIERCE MEMORIAL LECTURES

AT CORNELL UNIVERSITY, OCTOBER 1968

The Origin and Evolution of the I.L.O.
and Its Role in the World Community

The Frank W. Pierce Memorial Lectureship, at
the New York State School of Industrial and
Labor Relations at Cornell University, is made
possible through the generosity of the Teagle
Foundation, Incorporated.

David A. Morse

The Origin and Evolution of the I.L.O. and Its Role in the World Community

DAVID A. MORSE

Director-General of the I.L.O.

New York State School of Industrial and Labor
Relations, Cornell University, Ithaca, New York

1969

Copyright © 1969 by Cornell University

All rights reserved

Library of Congress Catalog Card Number: 68-66942

Price: $3.50

ORDER FROM

Distribution Center, New York State School
of Industrial and Labor Relations,
Cornell University, Ithaca, New York 14850

PRINTED IN THE UNITED STATES OF AMERICA
BY THE W. F. HUMPHREY PRESS, INC.

Foreword

THIS history of the International Labor Organization, by David A. Morse, its distinguished Director-General, is the third in the Pierce Memorial Lectureship series, supported by the Teagle Foundation, in memory of Frank W. Pierce, a graduate of Cornell University in 1916 and himself a pioneer in industrial relations during his career with the Standard Oil Company (New Jersey). Mr. Pierce had been a member of the Advisory Council of the New York State School of Industrial and Labor Relations from 1953 to 1956, and a member of the Cornell University Council from 1951 to 1962. The first series of lectures was presented by Professor Nicholas Kaldor, Cambridge University; the second by President John Coleman of Haverford College.

These lectures by Director-General Morse were delivered at the New York State School of Industrial and Labor Relations, Cornell University, on October 15, 16, and 17, 1968.

The I.L.O. was established fifty years ago under the League of Nations, and has continued to serve the world as one of the specialized agencies of the United Nations. It has a unique structure, with tripartite representation from the participating nations; that is, with labor, management, and government representatives.

Mr. Morse was elected to the post of Director-General in June 1948, and has held that office since, having been unanimously reelected at each periodic election. His tenure of office, the longest of any Director-General, in itself is recognition of his remarkable contributions to the evolution of the I.L.O.

VERNON H. JENSEN, *Associate Dean*
New York State School of
Industrial and Labor Relations

Contents

FIRST LECTURE

Origins and Historical Development of the I.L.O.: 1919-1948

NEXT year we shall be celebrating the 50th anniversary of the International Labor Organization. This event will give those of us who serve the Organization, as well as the government, employers, and workers of the 118 countries which are its members, an opportunity to look back over its eventful history, to take stock of its present position, and to sketch its likely development in the foreseeable future.

I was, therefore, pleased when I received an invitation to deliver these lectures, since I felt this to be an excellent opportunity to trace, however briefly, the history of the I.L.O., to reflect on its aims and purposes, to measure the ground it has covered in its fifty years of existence, and finally to consider the role it is called upon to play in the world community of today and tomorrow.

At the same time, I was rather concerned by the challenge. In attempting, in three brief lectures, to trace the history of the I.L.O. and to assess its role in the world, I shall of course have to be highly selective. I shall try in a few broad strokes to convey an impression, as I see it, of the long-term significance of this half-century of international endeavour.

Origin

Let me begin with the Paris Peace Conference, which assembled in January 1919, two months after the armistice which put an end to hostilities in the First World War.

At one of the first sessions, the Conference set up a Commission on International Labor Legislation, of which Samuel Gompers, the first president of the American Federation of Labor, was chairman. Some of the delegates may have thought it rather surprising that one of the first acts of the Peace Conference should relate to labor; but there was general recognition that the ferment and instability which characterized the world of labor and industry in 1918 and 1919, particularly in Europe, called for immediate and constructive action.

The Commission, which was composed of representatives of nine countries,[1] had to deal with the

---

[1]Belgium, Cuba, Czechoslovakia, France, Italy, Japan, Poland, United Kingdom, United States. James T. Shotwell, *Origins of the International Labour Organisation*, vol. 1, pp. 128–129.

4

important question of whether it should propose that there be included in the Peace Treaty a full-fledged Constitution of a permanent international labor organization, or whether it should simply recommend the inclusion of a general declaration of principles, a sort of Labor Charter.

It finally decided to formulate the Constitution of an organization which would be designed to examine new problems of labor and industry as they arose and to assist in finding solutions for them. In addition, but only secondarily, it agreed to approve a list of general principles.

The Commission's report consisted of two parts, one containing the Constitution of the proposed International Labor Organization, including provisions concerning its relations with the League of Nations; the other, the list of general principles on labor matters. The report was adopted by the Peace Conference during April 1919. Both parts were subsequently embodied in the Treaty of Versailles.

Although the Paris Peace Conference is remembered mainly for its short-lived policies and decisions on political and economic affairs, its main decision in the field of social policy—the establishment of the I.L.O.—continues today to have a far-reaching impact on the world.

Before going on to describe the Constitution of the I.L.O., I should like to glance for a moment back into history.

By a curious historical coincidence, it was almost exactly a century before the Paris Conference that for the first time proposals for action in each nation to regulate conditions of labor were submitted to an international conference by the Welsh-Scottish industrialist, Robert Owen, at the Congress of Aix-la-Chapelle. At the time, Owen was a voice crying in the wilderness, but in the years that followed other employers advocated action to the same end, Hindley in England and Legrand in France. It was their realization that efforts in the direction of national legislation to regulate conditions of labor would be impeded by the lack of coordinated international action in the field which led Hindley and Legrand in the 1830's and 1840's to advocate international labor treaties or conventions.

On the side of the workers, the International Working Men's Association, the First International, formed in 1864, the Second International, formed in 1889, and the International Federation of Trade Unions, which traced its origins to a conference held in 1901 and which was formally constituted in 1913, all voiced in different ways the international aspirations of the workers to improve the lot of working men everywhere.

Governments also, influenced by currents of economic and social thought in the nineteenth century, as well as pressures exerted by or on behalf of workers, had taken some action. In 1890, after earlier initiatives by Colonel Frey, president of the Swiss Confederation, an international conference on conditions of labor was convened in Berlin by Chancellor Bismarck.

Thus employers, workers, and governments all played a part, though separately, in the evolution of the concept of international action for the promotion of labor standards. All these initiatives had been inspired by men who were genuinely concerned with the hardships which nineteenth-century industrialization and economic competition inflicted upon workers. In 1900, very largely as a result of this growing "social conscience" in European countries, the International Association for Labor Legislation, a nongovernmental organization which received financial support from interested governments, was established. This organization, although its work had little immediate effect on national legislation, can be considered a direct forerunner of the I.L.O.

Near the end of the First World War, when the Allied governments were making preparations for the Peace Conference, they had to take due account of the international workers' conferences, held during the war in Leeds, Stockholm, and Berne, which had urged and resolved that the terms of peace should ensure to the workers minimum guarantees in regard to labor legislation and trade union rights, in recognition of the signal services rendered during the war by the workers, both in the factories and on the battlefield.

All this explains why the Commission on International Labor Legislation was set up, at the Paris Peace Conference, and why the report of this Commission was unanimously adopted by the Conference.

Structure and Mandate

The Constitution of the I.L.O. defines the aims of the Organization and formulates its structure. The basic structure is simple: the members of the I.L.O. are sovereign States; they meet at least once a year at a Conference, to which each member is entitled to send a tripartite delegation consisting of four delegates, two representing the government, the other two representing, respectively, the employers and the workers of the country. A Governing Body has general responsibility for coordinating the activities of the Organization into an overall program which can be adjusted to take account of changing needs and priorities. Third, there is an International Labor Office, with a permanent international staff, headed by a Director-General.

Simple as this structure is, it includes several innovations which were startling in 1919, and which remain unique today. In particular, the I.L.O. provides for the representatives of management and labor a status equal to that of representatives of governments. In the Conference and in the Governing Body, employers' and workers' delegates sit side by side with government delegates and enjoy equal rights. Unique in this respect among international organizations, the I.L.O. has owed its vigor and vitality, and a large measure of its success, to the balanced cooperation of governments, management, and labor in developing its policies and programs. I have more to say in Lecture II about the strength which its tripartite structure has imparted to the I.L.O., as well as some of the problems to which the structure has given rise.

The mandate given to the I.L.O. in the Constitution is broad and challenging. It is the promotion of: "Lasting Peace Through Social Justice." This aim is to be attained through action to improve the conditions of life and labor of the working men and women of the world. In order to accomplish this aim, the I.L.O. was assigned two main functions: to establish international labor standards, and to collect and distribute information on labor and industrial conditions.

Under the terms of the Constitution, these international standards are to be adopted by the International Labor Conference in the form of Conventions and Recommendations. All member States of the Organization are under an obligation to submit Conventions and Recommendations to their competent national authorities. When Conventions are ratified they become binding on the ratifying country, and a framework for enforcement machinery to supervise implementation of Conventions is provided. Recommendations are not open to ratification; as the name suggests, they are to provide guidance for national legislation, collective negotiation, and administrative action. In 1919 these provisions represented a new venture both in law and in politics.

The framers of the Constitution did not conceive the role of the I.L.O. as a narrowly legal or technical one. According to the words of the preamble, the High Contracting Parties, in agreeing to the Constitution, were "moved by sentiments of justice and humanity." These principles of justice and humanity were to be guiding lights for the Organization; its ultimate purpose was to contribute to rebuilding a world at peace, which would develop not only in material prosperity but also in respect for human dignity and spiritual values.

The Early Years (1919–1921)

The new organization lost no time in getting to work. On 29 October 1919 the first session of the International Labor Conference opened in Washington. Washington had been named in the Peace Treaty as the meeting place of the first session of the Conference on the invitation of President Woodrow Wilson. Unfortunately, a series of setbacks to collaboration between the I.L.O. and the United States had occurred during the months before the opening of the Conference. The United States had not ratified the Peace Treaty; it was a member neither of the League of Nations nor of the I.L.O.; and the President has suffered a physical breakdown. Nevertheless, the Conference pursued its task and adopted six Conventions and six Recommendations. These detailed international agreements covered a wide range of problems, including the eight-hour day and 48-hour week, unemployment, maternity protection in industry and commerce, night work of women and young persons, and minimum age for employment in industry. The Conference thus laid the foundations of a system of international labor legislation far in advance of anything previously considered feasible.

A few weeks later the Governing Body, appointed by the Washington Conference, met to take the necessary steps to organize the International Labor Office, and appointed as its first Director, Albert Thomas, one of the most outstanding figures in the history of the French socialist movement, who had been Minister of Munitions of France during the war. Thus only five months after the signature of the Peace Treaty, the International Labor Organization was already actively at work. The I.L.O. was, in fact, the first of the political, social, and judicial institutions provided for in the Peace Treaty to come into effective operation.

Less than seven months after the close of the Washington Conference, the second session of the Conference was held in the Italian seaport of Genoa. This session was concerned with conditions of employment at sea, and although it failed to agree on a Convention on hours of work, it adopted three Conventions and four Recommendations on conditions of work at sea and in inland navigation. A year later in Geneva, the third session of the Conference, which was devoted in the main to problems of labor in agriculture, adopted seven Conventions and eight Recommendations. Thus, in less than two years the Conference had adopted, with a view to action by its member States, no fewer than 34 international agreements.

The same expeditiousness was demonstrated by the International Labor Office in launching an ambitious program of publications. From 1920 onward the I.L.O. began to issue periodical publications and several other series of documents. The periodicals included the *Official Bulletin,* containing the official records of the actions taken by the Organization; the monthly *International Labour Review,* containing articles, both factual and theoretical, on trends in social policy; and a newspaper containing news about current events in the field of labor and industry. In addition to these periodicals, translations and reprints of labor laws were issued in the *Legislative Series;* research studies were published in the series entitled *Studies and Reports;* and other special publications were issued from time to time.

In the meantime the Director had recruited an international team to form the nucleus of the Secretariat of the Organization. The International Labor Office, after having been located in London for a few months, had by midsummer of 1920 been established in Geneva.[2]

In those early years, the image of the I.L.O. was established as one of boundless enthusiasm and explosive energy.

Difficulties and Successes (1922–1932)

Inevitably, opposition began to develop, perhaps as a reaction to the very enthusiasm and energy demonstrated by the young Organization. The great optimism which had prevailed immediately following the end of the war had given way to doubt, and indeed often to deep pessimism. It was by no means clear that Allied victory had in fact made the world "safe for democracy." Employers and workers were not always finding in cooperation the solution of their conflicts. Fresh political tensions were mount-

---

[2]The I.L.O. was actually established in Geneva before the League of Nations, which came toward the end of year. League of Nations, "Procès-Verbal of the Tenth Session of the Council, held in Brussels, 20th October, 1920– 28th October, 1920," *passim; Annuaire de la Société des Nations,* 1920–1927, preparé sous la direction de Georges Otlik, vol. 1, p. 230.

ing. Unemployment was soaring as the world economy reeled under alternating glut and famine, boom and slump.

Within the Organization grave difficulties were emerging. To many it seemed essential to place a curb on the I.L.O.—to restrict its powers and to limit its activities.

In the first place, it was felt that the Conference had gone too far and too fast in the output of Conventions and Recommendations. National governments and national parliaments could not give proper consideration to 16 Conventions and 18 Recommendations adopted in less than two years. In reviewing the progress of ratifications of those Conventions, Albert Thomas, the activist *par excellence,* noted the disappointing results and reached the conclusion that overproduction of Conventions and Recommendations must cease; a breathing space was needed.

In the second place, the publications program of the Office became a target for bitter criticism, and the I.L.O. had to learn an important lesson, namely, that it was not enough for its research in fact to be objective and impartial; it had to be recognized as being objective and impartial. With that end in view, the I.L.O. adopted the practice of seeking independent guarantees of impartiality by providing for consultation of small committees of outside experts when particularly controversial questions were being investigated.

At the same time, efforts were being made to restrict the competence of the I.L.O. In 1921 the French government took the position that the I.L.O. was not competent to deal with agricultural matters and the Permanent Court of International Justice was requested to give an advisory opinion on the question. The Court found that the competence of the I.L.O. did extend to international regulation of the conditions of labor of persons employed in agriculture. In reaching that conclusion the Court rejected a restrictive interpretation of the Constitution. The same attitude was displayed by the Court in two subsequent advisory opinions handed down in 1922 and in 1926, also relating to questions of competence of the I.L.O. Attempts to induce the Court to restrict the scope of action of the I.L.O. therefore failed, and the Court's decisions were generally accepted as authorizing the broad interpretation which Albert Thomas and his colleagues had been giving to the Constitution.

Another serious difficulty which emerged at this time was the financing of the Organization. Under the Constitution, the I.L.O. was dependent on the League of Nations for its financing. On the other hand, in all matters of general policy the Constitution provided for the absolute independence of the I.L.O. Obviously, this arrangement contained the seeds of serious difficulties. Nevertheless, a workable system of budgetary and financial relations was quickly developed, which, while respecting the autonomy of the I.L.O., provided for the adoption of its budget by the Assembly of the League. In 1923, however, a group of governments which favored restricting the I.L.O.'s activities developed both in the Governing Body of the I.L.O. and in the Assembly of the League. This group sought to restrict the budget of the I.L.O. and a massive reduction was effected. The restricted budget for 1924, approximately $1,400,000, became established as a standard level for the I.L.O., and throughout the balance of the interwar period the budget remained stabilized at approximately the same figure. The stabilization of the budget naturally gave rise to a period of stabilization and consolidation in the programs and activities of the I.L.O.

The Conference continued to meet every year, but the output of Conventions and Recommendations was drastically reduced. The twelve sessions between 1922 and 1931 adopted 15 Conventions, one less than the number adopted at the first three sessions, and 21 Recommendations, only three more than the number adopted at the first three sessions. Although this limitation of the standard-setting work of the I.L.O. was not everywhere welcomed, two definite advantages resulted.

First, time was given to national governments and parliaments to devote adequate attention to applying the provisions of the international agreements in national laws and regulations. More and more countries ratified I.L.O. Conventions, and I.L.O. standards began to exercise an effective influence in the improvement of conditions of life and work throughout the world.

Second, action was taken in 1926 to implement the constitutional provisions on the supervision of the application of ratified Conventions. This was a delicate question and the Conference was at first reluctant to tackle it. But when at last it decided to seize the nettle, it seized it firmly. It decided that in future each session of the Conference would appoint a committee to examine the reports presented by governments on the application of Conventions ratified by them, and invited the Governing Body to appoint an independent and prestigious Committee of Experts to examine the reports and to submit its own report to the Conference, for consideration along with the reports from governments. These arrangements were put into practice in the following year, and formed the basis of the system of implementation of labor standards which has since been developed.

Stabilization and consolidation also characterized the information work of the I.L.O. The publications program remained virtually unchanged. If the quantity was somewhat reduced, this was compensated by an improvement in quality, and the I.L.O. began to gain recognition as the world authority in regard to statistical and other information on conditions of labor and industry. In at least one instance during this period, new ground was broken in the research program.

In 1929, thanks to assistance from Industrial Relations Counsellors of New York, I.L.O. staff members began to visit important industrial and commercial undertakings in Europe and North America and to prepare reports on labor-management relations within those undertakings. These reports, which were published by the I.L.O., proved to be very popular, demonstrating a real desire among both employers and workers to learn more about how day-by-day problems analogous to their own were being handled in other countries.

I should emphasize that the stabilization of the I.L.O.'s basic programs during this period in no sense implied stagnation. Albert Thomas continued to inspire his staff to take advantage of every opportunity to promote the objectives of the I.L.O. He was a great believer in the "policy of presence," and the missions he undertook throughout the world, at a time when travelling was more difficult and time-consuming than it is now, are a matter of history. He was indefatigable, as was his staff, in establishing and maintaining relations with Ministers and leaders of employers' associations and trade unions and with others concerned with social policy and progress. Those who knew him remember him as a statesman, administrator, orator, and constructive initiator, whose vision was matched by his realism. When he died suddenly in 1932, in the prime of his life, a legendary epoch closed in the history of the I.L.O.

Facing the Gathering Storm (1932–1938)

To succeed Albert Thomas, the Governing Body appointed Harold Butler. Butler had been Deputy Director from the outset, and before that had been intimately concerned with the drafting of the I.L.O. Constitution in the Commission on International Labor Legislation at the Peace Conference. Upon taking office, Butler found himself faced with the immediate problem of what action should be taken by the I.L.O. to contribute to lifting the world economy out of the Great Depression. Unemployment had by then reached astronomical figures; in some industrial countries more than one-third of the working force was unemployed. Every branch of industry and commerce was affected. Governments multiplied restrictions on foreign trade and foreign exchange. The economic and social security of workers was being progressively undermined.

The workers in many countries believed that one solution to the problem of unemployment lay in reducing hours of work so as to spread available employment more widely. They, therefore, pressed in the International Labor Conference for the adoption of international agreements to reduce hours of work.

But the Conference was divided on the matter. While the workers received support from certain governments, the employers were opposed, and their attitude was shared by other governments. In these circumstances, though the question of hours of work figured in one form or another on the agenda of every Conference until 1939, the results were meagre.[3]

Butler supported every possible means available to the I.L.O. for contributing to solving the unemployment problem, and even attempted to launch an international public works program to relieve unemployment. In his reports to the Conference from 1933 to 1938 he continued to stress the interdependence of social, economic, and financial policy; in his view, a cure for unemployment could not be found in isolation from considerations of economic and financial policy.

Another significant characteristic of Harold Butler's term of office, which was to have great significance for the future development and ultimately the survival of the I.L.O., was the importance he attached to broadening the geographical horizons of the Organization. The world outside Europe was coming to play an increasingly important role in international affairs, but this was not fully reflected in the membership of the I.L.O. In particular, Butler

---

[3]The 40 Hour-Week Convention was adopted by the I.L.O. in 1935. To date there have been only four ratifications of this Convention: New Zealand, U.S.S.R., Byelorussia, Ukraine.

never ceased to look forward to the day when the United States would become a member of the I.L.O. The obstacles to this were formidable, however, as the I.L.O. was still constitutionally linked to the League of Nations, and the United States was determined to have no association with the League. But the election of President Franklin Roosevelt in 1932, and the implementation of the President's New Deal policies, opened up the possibility of reconsideration of the decision of the United States in 1919 to take no part in the work of the I.L.O. The social policies of the United States came more closely into line with those advocated by the I.L.O.[4] Roosevelt knew Harold Butler, whom he had met in Washington in 1919 on the occasion of the first International Labor Conference; and his Secretary of Labor, Frances Perkins, was thoroughly acquainted with the I.L.O. and sympathetic to its aims. Butler, on his side, did everything possible to facilitate the entry of the United States. In 1934, ways and means were found to overcome the constitutional difficulties, I.L.O. membership was approved by Congress, despite some

[4]The I.L.O.'s work in the social security field, for example, appears to have been of some relevance and use in the development of the social security system in the United States. In 1936, the Chief of the I.L.O.'s Social Insurance Section came to Washington, at the request of the U.S. Government, for consultation in regard to certain technical problems arising out of the new Social Security Act. *First Report of the International Labour Organisation to the United Nations,* p. 128.

isolationist opposition, and the United States became a member of the I.L.O. in time to participate in the Conference in June.

Concurrently, steps were taken to improve the relations of the I.L.O. with its existing members from outside Europe—Canada, India, Australia, New Zealand, South Africa, and others. In 1936 Egypt entered the I.L.O. In the same year, as a result of the first I.L.O. regional Conference—a Conference of its American members held at Santiago de Chile—relations between the I.L.O. and its Latin American members became more intimate and more effective.

In the meantime, an important amendment of the Constitution, which had been adopted as early as 1922, but the implementation of which had been prevented by Italy's exercise of her veto power within the Council of the League, finally came into effect in 1934, when Italy agreed to ratify the amendment in return for certain changes in the procedural rules of the Conference. This constitutional amendment made it possible for the Conference in 1934 to elect a greatly enlarged Governing Body which gave substantially increased representation to countries from outside Europe. Within the Office, an Overseas Section was organized to ensure that greater attention should be paid to special problems affecting those countries.[5]

---

[5]Reference should also be made to the work of the I.L.O. between 1920 and 1939 in helping to improve living and working

It was clear that the world beyond the confines of Europe was becoming of much greater importance than previously, and this growing importance was reflected in the changes in the membership and structure of the I.L.O. which I have just described. The fact that the I.L.O. was able to adapt itself to this fact proved to be of decisive importance for its survival during the war that was shortly to follow. It also provided a basis for the reconstruction and transformation of the Organization after the war.

Several factors were involved in the resignation of Butler, which occurred in 1938.[6] One of the factors, to which he attributed great importance in his memoirs, concerned the maintenance of a truly independent international civil service. As this has been a central preoccupation of each Director of the I.L.O. since the earliest days of the Organization, it may be

conditions in dependent territories, and thus to pave the way for the ultimate independence of these territories. The I.L.O. participated in an advisory capacity in the work of the Permanent Mandates Commission and undertook studies of the conditions of labor in dependent territories, and the Conference adopted four Conventions and five Recommendations dealing with forced labor, recruitment of workers, contracts of employment, and penal sanctions, all with particular relevance to the protection of workers in dependent territories. *ibid.,* pp. 94–95.

[6]Butler subsequently served as Warden of Nuffield College, Oxford, from 1939 to 1943, Commissioner for Civil Defence for the Southern Region of the United Kingdom from 1939 to 1941, and Minister at the British Embassy in Washington from 1942 to 1946. He died in 1951. *Who Was Who, 1951–1960.*

useful to mention here that Butler, by his own account, decided to resign rather than appoint an official in whom he had no confidence but whose candidature for an important position in the Organization was persistently pressed by his government. He felt the matter involved a vital question of principle, and that resignation was the only course he could take when he found himself unable to prevail upon the government in question to change its position. Pressures analogous to those which resulted in Butler's resignation were not a new phenomenon for the I.L.O. in 1938, and, I might add parenthetically, have occurred from time to time since then. Each Director has had to deal with these pressures in his own way, but each has done his utmost to establish and maintain the principle of the complete independence of the I.L.O. official, to which each new official adheres when he takes up employment by subscribing to a declaration of loyalty which provides that he shall not "seek or accept instructions in regard to the performance of his duties from any government or other authority external to the I.L.O."

Riding the Storm (1939–1943)

Butler's successor was John G. Winant, who had been Governor of New Hampshire and was the first chairman of the United States Social Security Board; he had also served as an Assistant Director of the I.L.O.

Albert Thomas, first Director, 1919–1932

Harold Butler, Director, 1932–1938

John Winant, Director, 1939–1941

Edward Phelan, Director, 1941–1948

Samuel Gompers and Albert Thomas at the Paris Peace Conference, 1919

An I.L.O. Seminar in Workers' Education, held at Douala, Cameroon, 1963

An I.L.O. Metal Industry Training Project, held in Taiwan

Though Winant was unwilling to accept that war was inevitable, he recognized that the risks of war were daily increasing. Certain elementary precautions were taken by the Governing Body which appointed a small Emergency Committee, authorized, if the Governing Body should be unable to meet, to take action in its name. Nevertheless, the essential activities of the Organization continued uninterrupted, and in June 1939 the Conference met as usual.

When the war broke out that September, it seemed at first that the I.L.O. might be able to continue its work in Geneva, but in May 1940 the sudden westward flow of battle isolated Switzerland. If the I.L.O. was to continue to operate and indeed survive, it was urgently necessary to transfer its working centre away from Geneva. Careful preparations for such a move had been made by the Governing Body's Emergency Committee during the months preceding the war, on the basis of which Winant was able to take the important decision to find a refuge for the I.L.O. outside Europe. His original intention was to find such a refuge in the United States. But, however sympathetic President Roosevelt might personally have been to this suggestion, he was probably unwilling, at the time, to do battle with domestic isolationist opinion on that issue. Consequently, shouldering the burden of responsibility for decision, Winant left in Geneva a small caretaker and liaison group, and successfully negotiated arrangements for the establishment in Montreal of the working nucleus of the I.L.O. staff. In these negotiations Winant was greatly aided by his friendship with MacKenzie King, the Canadian Prime Minister. At that time and thereafter, Winant's action was recognized as having maintained the continuity and as having preserved the essential freedom of operation of the Organization.

In 1941 Winant resigned to accept appointment as wartime Ambassador of the United States in London, and Edward Phelan, the Deputy Director, became Acting Director. Phelan, an Irishman who had been in the British Civil Service, had participated with Butler in the preparation of the draft I.L.O. Constitution, and had entered the International Labor Office at its very inception.

Realizing the need for an early meeting of the members of the Organization, even though war conditions rendered impossible a regular session of the International Labor Conference, Phelan undertook the necessary consultations and a Conference was convened in October 1941 in New York, with the closing sitting taking place in the White House at President Roosevelt's invitation. Attended by high-ranking representatives of governments, employers, and workers, the Conference emphasized "the desirability of associating the I.L.O. with the planning and application of measures of reconstruction," and urged that the I.L.O. should "be in a position to give authoritative expression to the social objectives confided to it in the rebuilding of a peaceful world upon the basis of improved labor standards, economic advancement and social security." Thus, even in the midst of the world's severest crisis, there was a determination that the I.L.O. should not only survive but also play an active and constructive role.

In the years of endurance that followed, the I.L.O. did all that it could do, with its nucleus of staff and its skeleton budget. Its standard-setting work had to be suspended as no International Labor Conference could meet, but advisory missions on social insurance were sent to countries in Latin America and elsewhere.[7] The information program was pursued through the *International Labour Review* and various special publications. Close contact was maintained with Washington and London, where plans were already being developed for a new international organization to succeed the League of Nations. In 1943 the Governing Body courageously decided to convene a regular session of the International Labor Conference for the following year. That Conference was destined to constitute a milestone in the history of the Organization in that it was there that the new outlook of the I.L.O. was determined.

[7]During this period, the I.L.O. sent technical missions in the field of social insurance to advise and consult with requesting governments in Venezuela, Ecuador, Bolivia, Chile, Costa Rica, Mexico, Haiti, India, Egypt, and Turkey. *First Report of the International Labour Organisation to the United Nations,* pp. 128–130.

27

The New Outlook (1944–1948)

Meeting in Philadelphia in April–May 1944, during the height of the Second World War, the Conference, composed of government, employer, and worker delegates coming from 41 countries, agreed on seven Recommendations designed to deal with emerging problems in the fields of social security and employment, as well as social policy in dependent territories. More important, it adopted a Declaration of basic principles. "That Declaration," said President Roosevelt, in an address at the White House, "sums up the aspirations of an epoch which has known two world wars. I confidently believe that future generations will look upon it as a landmark in world thinking." Referring to the American Declaration of Independence, he said, "The Declaration which you have formulated in Philadelphia may well acquire a similar significance. In it you have reaffirmed principles which are the essential bulwarks of any permanent peace."

The Declaration of Philadelphia laid down two basic principles: first, that it must be the central aim of national and international policy to achieve conditions in which all men and women can pursue their material well-being and their spiritual development in freedom and dignity, economic security, and equal opportunity; and second, that all national and international efforts should be judged in the light of whether or not they help to further this aim. The I.L.O. was entrusted with a special responsibility to the peoples of the world to examine and consider international economic and financial policies and measures in order to ensure that social policy was made a dominant concern and the welfare of the people a central objective.

In the Declaration the I.L.O.'s original mandate was formulated in more comprehensive and positive terms. The earlier concept of protecting workers against the hazards of sickness, accident, and old age was replaced by a more affirmative ideal of social security to provide a basic income, comprehensive medical care, and effective promotion of health and well-being. The aim of preventing unemployment was restated in terms of fostering full employment and thus contributing to higher living standards. The problem of working conditions was no longer considered solely in relation to the removing of specific hardships but was placed in the broader context of policies governing wages, working hours, and other matters which were to be designed to ensure a fairer sharing of the fruits of economic and social progress. Other prewar objectives were made more comprehensive; the concept of freedom of association now included the recognition of the right to bargain collectively and the promotion of labor-management cooperation in improving productive efficiency.

Not the least significant result of the Conference was the evidence it provided of the unswerving support of the I.L.O. on the part of both workers and employers. Some governments had indicated a preference for replacing the old I.L.O. with an entirely new organization. The workers' and employers' delegates, on the other hand, were unwilling to acquiesce in the dismantling of an organization in which they enjoyed a status equal to that of governments. Their main concern, and that of many governments, was rather to improve the I.L.O.'s capacity to face up to the new challenges presented by the postwar world.

Philadelphia thus marked the opening of a new era in the history of the Organization. After the uncertainties of the long wartime years, Philadelphia symbolized the rebirth of steadfast confidence in the mission of the I.L.O. It permitted a start to be made in reconstructing the I.L.O., which could begin again to take its place in the mainstream of world affairs.

The years 1945 and 1946 were decisive for the I.L.O. In June 1945 the Charter of the United Nations was adopted at San Francisco, and the new pattern of postwar international organization began to emerge more clearly. But the place of the I.L.O. in that system had not yet been defined. At San Francisco the representatives of the I.L.O. had been received coldly; there were pressures for a clean sweep not only of the League of Nations, but also of all the organizations linked with it. The I.L.O. was still constitutionally associated with the League, and some delegates at San Francisco doubted whether the I.L.O. could succeed in disentangling itself. Moreover, it was felt by some governments that the World Federation of Trade Unions, which was likewise created in 1945, could assume many of the I.L.O.'s functions with respect to labor and social policy in the United Nations system, and that consequently the I.L.O. had become superfluous. As a result the United Nations Charter contained no reference to the I.L.O.

In October, at the invitation of General de Gaulle, the International Labor Conference met in Paris. The Conference, assembled in the city in which the Constitution of the I.L.O. had been adopted 26 years before, set to work to revise that Constitution to meet the demands of the postwar era. In amending the Constitution, the Conference deleted the provisions concerning relations with the League of Nations in respect of membership and finance, and added similar provisions on relations with the United Nations. These new provisions were not very elaborate as it was felt that details on relations with the United Nations should be spelled out in an agreement to be negotiated with that organization.

In the early months of 1946 negotiations began between the I.L.O. and the United Nations, at first on the Secretariat level and later between the I.L.O. Negotiating Delegation and the U.N. Committee on

Negotiations with Specialized Agencies. The successful conclusion of these negotiations, resulting in a formal detailed Agreement, owed much to the mutual confidence and comprehension of the two chairmen, Sir Guildhaume Myrddin-Evans of the United Kingdom, on behalf of the I.L.O., and Sir Ramaswami Mudaliar of India, on behalf of the United Nations.

The Agreement was approved by the International Labor Conference in September 1946 and by the Assembly of the United Nations in December of the same year. It was the first agreement of this nature to be concluded between the United Nations and a specialized agency, and it served to a large extent as the model for subsequent agreements.

The same year, 1946, was also marked by an upsurge of activity in the traditional programs of the I.L.O. Two sessions of the Conference at Seattle and at Montreal added 13 Conventions and six Recommendations to the International Labor Code; the series of regional conferences was resumed with a session in Mexico City; and the publications program was vigorously expanded. The first meetings of the industrial committees were held. These committees, about which I shall have more to say in my lecture tomorrow, were established by the Governing Body on the proposal of Ernest Bevin, the then Minister of Labour of the United Kingdom, with the ambitious aim of providing a framework for international collective bargaining, on an industry-by-industry basis, in the reconstruction of the postwar economy.

Finally, the amendment of the Constitution was completed, involving significant changes in the structure and mandate of the I.L.O. For the first time the International Labor Conference adopted the budget of the Organization and the I.L.O. thus became financially autonomous.

In recognition of the services rendered by Edward Phelan, who as Acting Director since 1941 had, through foresight in direction, finesse in negotiation, and fidelity to the ideals of the Organization, guided it during the difficult war years, he was appointed Director-General. In the intervening time until his retirement in 1948, Phelan had the satisfaction of seeing the Organization grow in strength and influence.

The years 1947 and 1948 were marked by two major developments. First, in the area of international labor standards, Conventions were adopted at Conferences in Geneva (1947) and San Francisco (1948), on social policy in nonmetropolitan territories and on freedom of association and protection of the right to organize, thus crowning the endeavours of the prewar period in these fields. Second, the initial steps were taken in a program of assistance in solving postwar manpower problems which was a prelude to one of the most fruitful enterprises of the I.L.O. in the postwar era.

These two years may thus be regarded as both the epilogue of one stage in the history of the I.L.O. and the prologue to the succeeding stage. For the world was to change in the next few years in ways which could scarcely have been foreseen at the time. And the I.L.O. had to keep pace with these changes. In Lecture II, I examine how the I.L.O. faced up to the challenge of the 1950's and 1960's.

SECOND LECTURE

Response to the Needs of
a Rapidly Changing World:
1948-1968

IT IS now twenty years since I took up my functions as Director-General of the I.L.O.[1] These twenty years in the history of the I.L.O. have been characterized by a rapid growth of the Organization, and by a continuing process of transformation in its activities and its methods of work in response to the changing needs of a rapidly changing world.

The growth of the Organization in this period can be illustrated by some figures. The I.L.O.'s membership has more than doubled, rising from 55 States in 1948 to 118 today. The regular budget of the Organization has increased more than fivefold, from some

---

[1]Mr. Morse was elected Director-General of the I.L.O. in San Francisco on 12 June 1948 ("Minutes of the 105th Session of the Governing Body," pp. 14–15) and officially assumed office on 6 September 1948 (*Official Bulletin,* vol. 21, no. 3, December 31, 1948, p. 189).

$4.5 million in 1948 to nearly $25 million in 1968, and the over-all annual resources nearly tenfold by the addition of $20 million which is placed at the I.L.O.'s disposal from other sources, primarily the United Nations Development Program. The staff of the International Labor Office has increased from about 500 in 1948 to about 2,200 today.

But these figures give only the most superficial impression of the real changes that have taken place in the I.L.O. over the past twenty years. Let us look a little more closely at the facts behind the figures. And let us take the growth in the I.L.O.'s membership as a starting point.

Approach to Universality in Membership

From the outset, the aim of the founders and leaders of the I.L.O. has always been to make it a truly universal organization. In the preamble to the Constitution, the world-wide character of the Organization was thrice emphasized. Throughout its history, whenever a new Member has been admitted, its accession has been hailed as a further step toward the goal of complete universality.

In 1948 membership fell far short of that goal. On the one hand, several of the leading industrial countries, which had been Members before the war, were absent. On the other hand, vast areas of Africa and Asia had not yet attained independence and were, therefore, not eligible for membership.

However, after the "all-time low" in membership had been reached in 1942,[2] a movement of growth had begun and from 1948 onward that movement rapidly accelerated. Former Members returned, including in 1951 the Federal Republic of Germany and Japan and in 1954 the Soviet Union. During that period the I.L.O. also welcomed to membership several countries which had recently become independent. This group included Burma, Ceylon, Lebanon, and the Philippines in 1948, Israel in 1949, Indonesia and Vietnam in 1950, and Libya in 1952.

Thereafter, the annual trickle of new Members became a steady flow and then a flood, as more and more countries of Africa and other continents attained sovereignty. It has always been a matter of deep satisfaction to me that one of the first acts of so many countries on becoming independent has been to apply for membership in the I.L.O.

The development toward universality has not, of course, meant increasing uniformity among the I.L.O.'s Members. On the contrary, they represent the greatest possible diversity of race and ideology, and the widest possible range of social, economic, cultural, and political development. The I.L.O. must take into account the needs of all its Members and attempt to satisfy those needs and to guide national policies toward the fulfilment of its own primary aims.

---

[2] 46 Members.

39

This is not easy. Inevitably, there have been problems. The philosophical concept of unity in diversity is admirable in principle; but its practical application in international relations is far from simple.

This is particularly true of the I.L.O. with its tripartite membership. When the Soviet Union and other Eastern European countries renewed their active participation in the work of the I.L.O. in 1954, the Organization was brought to the brink of crisis. It was widely felt in employers' and workers' circles that the social system in the Socialist countries of Eastern Europe was incompatible with membership in the I.L.O., and that the presence of these countries in the Organization would shatter its very foundations. These countries are today still Members of the Organization; and even though the foundations of the I.L.O. can be said to remain as solid as ever, there are a number of unresolved problems concerning the status and participation of Socialist countries in the employers' and workers' groups, problems which do not arise in purely intergovernmental organizations such as the United Nations.

While tripartism has made universality difficult to achieve in practice, the development of the I.L.O. during the past twenty years would never have been possible had it not been for the presence of employers' and workers' representatives in the councils of the I.L.O. Tripartism has been and remains the very backbone of the I.L.O.; it has over the years helped to keep the I.L.O. in contact with the realities of social problems in all countries. The I.L.O. would be a much less effective instrument for dealing with labor matters at the international level if it did not have full representation of employers and workers in its councils. There has, therefore, never been any question of sacrificing tripartism to universality. The problem has been much more one of reconciling these two essential aspects of the I.L.O.'s structure. In this respect, some progress has been made.

The events of the past fourteen years have shown that tripartism and universality are not irreconcilable. Certain adjustments have had to be made in the procedures and methods of work of the Organization, and particularly of the International Labor Conference, to enable tripartite delegations from Socialist countries to participate effectively in our work. These adjustments have not met with the unanimous approval of the I.L.O.'s constituents. But at least they have enabled East and West to live together in the I.L.O., and there have been signs in recent years that hostile coexistence was beginning to give way to more active cooperation. I have more to say about this in Lecture III.

In 1963, the I.L.O. was brought to the brink of another crisis, this time in connection with the "apartheid" policy of the South African Government. In that year, following several years in which relations between the I.L.O. and South Africa had become increasingly difficult, matters came to a head. At a stormy session of the Conference the delegates of all the other African countries, many of which had just joined the I.L.O., supported by some other countries, withdrew in protest at the presence of a South African delegation at the Conference. They demanded that South Africa be expelled from the Organization. The Conference in the following year adopted unanimously a Declaration condemning the policy of apartheid, and also approved an amendment to the Constitution providing powers of suspension or expulsion; this amendment has not yet been ratified by the requisite number of I.L.O. Member States. In the meantime, South Africa had given formal notice of its intention to withdraw from membership, and its withdrawal took effect in 1966.

I mention these two episodes in the recent history of the Organization because they illustrate what is in my view an absolutely fundamental characteristic of the I.L.O.—its insistence that in all circumstances due process of law should be respected. On both occasions, feelings among the I.L.O.'s constituents ran very high, so high that the work of the Conference and of the Organization as a whole was almost brought to a standstill. But in spite of the intensity of feelings on both occasions, the problems were finally resolved within the framework of the procedures laid down in the I.L.O.'s Constitution, and not, as was to be feared, in defiance of due process of law. I believe that on both occasions the I.L.O. emerged strengthened as an instrument for international co-operation.

Changes in the Balance of Power

The increase in the number of Members of the I.L.O. has, of course, been accompanied by changes in the geographical distribution of its membership. In 1948 a majority of the I.L.O.'s Members was composed of the industrialized countries of Europe and America; today the developing countries of Africa and Asia comprise more than half the membership. These changes in the membership of the Organization have necessarily led to developments and adjustments in the International Labor Conference and the Governing Body.

The Conference has grown not only in size but also in status and stature. As I see it, the Conference has now become a fully representative body and can be viewed as a true world parliament of labor attended by Ministers of Labor and government officials, and by leaders of employers and workers from all parts of the world. Its annual sessions constitute a forum for the ventilation and discussion of the most pressing labor, social, and economic problems of the day. It serves as an opportunity for a review of world-wide social trends, and as a soundingboard from which delegates from all over the world may put forward their views on social questions. Furthermore, it offers vital guidance on the development of national and international policy in the social field.

The Governing Body, too, has become larger and more representative. It now has 48 members, including 24 government representatives, 12 employers, and 12 workers, as compared with 40 members prior to the most recent change in 1962.

The government group of the Governing Body is today broadly representative of all regions of the world. When the Organization was founded in 1919, nine of the 12 governments represented were European. Now the Government members comprise a balanced panel of four West Europeans, three East Europeans, two North Americans, four Latin Americans, five Asians, five Africans, and one representative from the Middle East.

The employer and worker members of the Governing Body are chosen in their personal capacity by electoral colleges consisting, respectively, of the employer and worker delegates at the Conference. There is still some dissatisfaction, often strongly expressed, that certain "tendencies" are not represented, or are inadequately represented, in the employers' and workers' groups of the Governing Body. For example, there are no Eastern European employer representatives in the employers' group of the Governing Body, nor are there any worker representatives from the Christian trade union movement

44

in the workers' group. However, the geographical distribution of the membership of both groups is much wider than in 1948. At the last Governing Body elections in 1966, for example, the representative of the trade unions of the Soviet Union was elected to the Governing Body. This is the first time that an Eastern European Socialist State has been represented on the workers' benches of the Governing Body.

Emphasis on Technical Cooperation Work

The changes in the composition of the policy-making organs of the I.L.O. have, as was to be expected, led to a profound transformation in the substance of the I.L.O.'s work.

In most of the I.L.O.'s member countries before 1948, the level of economic development, the form of social organization, and the nature of social problems were fairly similar. To improve conditions of work in this situation, the I.L.O. could accordingly rely mainly on international labor Conventions, which in many cases set fairly precise standards for labor legislation at the national level, concerning, for example, maximum normal hours of work, minimum number of holidays with pay, minimum ages of admission to employment, and so on.

The Organization was occasionally asked to advise governments on the implementation of international labor standards, and in the 1930's it even began to send out advisory missions to member countries for this purpose, chiefly in the field of social security. However, these tasks did not make a great call on the I.L.O.'s resources, which were mainly devoted to the collection and exchange of information, on the one hand, and to setting standards and supervising their application, on the other.

In 1948, when I assumed office as Director-General, it was clear to me that these activities, while important, were not enough. It seemed to me even then that one of the major issues in the world was the problem of underdevelopment, and that the traditional methods of I.L.O. action were inadequate to deal with that problem. I felt that, if the I.L.O. was to have the impact it should have on social policy in the world, it would have to become an *operational* organization.

Therefore, when I submitted my first report as Director-General to the International Labor Conference in 1949, I suggested that the experience accumulated by the Organization in the first thirty years of its existence could be used to the greatest advantage if it were made available immediately to the developing countries through the provision of technical assistance, on the spot, in the countries themselves.

This suggestion met with the agreement of the Conference and the Governing Body; its implementation in the ensuing years involved changes in program, organization, and structure which proved to be the first steps in a really radical transformation of the I.L.O.

On a modest scale to start with, money was made available and machinery was built up. An operational program was launched to provide assistance in the utilization of manpower resources, including organization of employment services, vocational guidance, and technical training.

At first, the resources for these activities were all provided out of the I.L.O.'s own budget.[3] However, in 1950, in response to a growing world-wide concern with the extreme poverty and backwardness of the countries of Asia, Africa, and Latin America, the United Nations launched the Expanded Program of Technical Assistance and the I.L.O. immediately became one of the executing organs of it. Accordingly, the resources available to the I.L.O. for direct assistance to its member States increased considerably.

Further resources for long-term projects became available in 1959 with the establishment of the United Nations Special Fund for Economic Development, of which the I.L.O. has been an executing agency since its inception. Finally, in 1966 the Ex-

---

[3]It should be noted that, in addition to the I.L.O.'s regular program, a special program to facilitate the placement in Latin America of emigrants from Europe was undertaken by the I.L.O. The O.E.E.C. made available $1,000,000 to finance this program.

panded Program and the Special Fund were merged in a single United Nations Development Program.

Thus, from its modest beginnings in 1948, technical cooperation (at first referred to as "advisory missions," then "technical assistance," before acquiring its present name which more truly reflects the spirit and character of the operation) has grown to become the most important of all the I.L.O.'s activities in terms of expenditure. In 1949, it represented $101,000, or approximately 2 percent of the I.L.O.'s total budget of $5,109,000. This year, in 1968, the I.L.O. is spending over $20,000,000 on technical cooperation activities in the field, or about 45 percent of the $45,000,000 available to it from all sources.

These figures will give some idea of the magnitude of I.L.O. technical cooperation and of the important role it plays in the I.L.O.'s activities today. But what has been the aim of the I.L.O's technical cooperation? What have we been attempting to achieve? How does technical cooperation fit in with the I.L.O.'s over-all program of activities?

By far the largest part of our technical cooperation activities—at least 60 percent—has been devoted to projects aimed at the development and fuller utilization of human resources in the developing countries. This has been, and still is, the I.L.O.'s main contribution to the attempts of these countries to modernize their economies, to accelerate the process of industrialization, in short to make themselves capable of providing higher standards of living for their people. For no one today will claim that these goals can be achieved merely by a massive injection of capital, however important that may be. Measures to build up a skilled, productive labor force constitute an indispensable element in any strategy for economic development. And for twenty years the I.L.O. has been assisting its member States, by direct practical action, in devising such measures.

Under a manpower program launched in 1948, technical advice was at first given primarily on vocational training to governments in Europe and Asia that were faced with shortages of skills. The emphasis in this program later shifted to migration, especially to deal with the problem of manpower surpluses in Europe and shortages elsewhere, particularly in Latin America.

The earliest projects specifically designed for developing countries were in 1951 and provided for the establishment of public employment services. However, it was realized that the main manpower problem in most underdeveloped areas is not how to match formal applications for employment with notified vacancies but how to provide more jobs, on the one hand, and to train more skilled workers, on the other. The I.L.O. has, therefore, promoted the systematic collection and analysis of information on employment trends and the use of the resulting knowledge in planning the development of human

49

resources as an integral part of the development of the economy as a whole. And this is now growing into a concerted attempt to raise levels of productive employment throughout the world, a subject to which I return in Lecture III.

Vocational training has throughout been one of the major components of the I.L.O.'s technical cooperation program. At first, the I.L.O.'s vocational training projects were mostly pilot schemes providing direct assistance in the training of limited numbers of skilled workers for industry. However, the scope of assistance increased greatly from 1959 onward, when the United Nations Special Fund made available much larger resources for so-called "preinvestment" activities. By now over half of the technical assistance organized by the I.L.O. relates to this sphere.

The I.L.O. has at the same time devoted much attention to the training of managers. Although the I.L.O.'s interest in management development goes back at least to 1927, when it lent its support to the establishment of the International Management Institute, its direct assistance to developing countries in that field dates from productivity missions that were sent to India and Israel in 1952. From these modest beginnings the I.L.O. productivity and management development activities have expanded to a point where they now constitute the largest international program in the world in that field, again largely financed by the United Nations Development Program.

In recent years, a major emphasis in the I.L.O.'s technical cooperation work has been on development of human resources and improvement of living conditions in rural areas. This has been increasingly recognized as necessary since the process of development has tended in most developing countries to bypass rural areas. And, conversely, the backwardness of agriculture has been one of the major obstacles to balanced economic development.

The I.L.O.'s technical cooperation has also been directed at facilitating adjustment to the new forms of society which are gradually emerging in the developing countries. People who are leaving their traditional environment to live and work in a new industrial society must be given an objective understanding of the conditions in which they will have to live and work. Furthermore, social institutions must be created through which they can develop new social relationships and cope with the problems they will inevitably encounter.

To this end, the I.L.O. has for some years been helping countries develop new institutions and social policies by assisting in drafting labor legislation; in strengthening government services to administer and implement this legislation; in building up machinery for the resolution of industrial conflict and for regulating relations between unions and management; in training responsible trade union leadership; and in devising appropriate social security schemes and wage policies which aim at ensuring a fair distribution of the fruits of development without imposing an excessive burden on the economy.

The essential feature of the technical cooperation activities of the I.L.O., like those of all United Nations agencies, has been that they have represented a truly cooperative endeavour. For technical cooperation is not a give-away scheme; a substantial portion of the cost of each project is borne by the recipient country. Moreover, an essential feature of these projects is the close association with the I.L.O. instructors or experts of national personnel appointed by the country concerned.

It is a central principle of international technical cooperation that a country receiving assistance should, from the very outset, collaborate actively with the mission by associating its own nationals with it and by sharing in the cost. Self-help is the key to the success of technical cooperation. The fundamental aim of the whole technical cooperation enterprise is to provide the countries concerned with the "know-how" to enable them to assume as quickly as possible full responsibility for the implementation of each project.

This aim has not always been achieved. There have been cases where, after a project has been completed and the experts' recommendations transmitted to the government, nothing further has happened. Perhaps political changes have taken place in the country, and the new government has had no interest in implementing the recommendations. Or perhaps the money needed for carrying on the work could not be found. Or perhaps the recommendations have simply been put away and forgotten.

There have been occasions, too, when the I.L.O. has been at fault. Our experts have not always been of a sufficiently high calibre; even where they were highly qualified, they have not always been able to adapt to the environment of the country of their assignment. On occasion, experts have been unable to establish close working relationships with the national personnel with whom they were collaborating. Happily, however, such cases of failure have been relatively few. Examples of projects which have had a lasting and beneficial effect are far more numerous.

But the question which preoccupies the I.L.O. and its member States is not the number of successes and failures recorded, but rather the ways in which the effectiveness and impact of our projects could be increased. In this respect, I would mention some recent developments in the I.L.O's technical cooperation which are making it a more powerful and effective weapon for economic development and social progress.

One major trend in technical cooperation is toward longer-term, more comprehensive projects, closely geared to national development plans. In the early days of technical assistance, governments used to request assistance in very limited fields and for a very short duration—often only two or three months. Such projects, while useful, often had little or no impact on the general problems of the country; they were rarely coordinated with other assistance provided by the I.L.O. or from other sources; often they had not been carefully conceived or planned; in many cases they did not correspond to the priority needs of the countries concerned; and in any case the projects were normally of such a short duration that the experts did not have time to do more than scratch the surface.

With the launching of the United Nations Special Fund in 1959, it became possible to implement much longer-term projects specifically designed to create conditions which would encourage investment and thus stimulate economic growth. At the same time, as countries have adopted, and acquired experience in, systems and methods of economic planning, it has increasingly become possible for them to identify more precisely their priority needs, and to integrate the assistance they receive more closely into development plans.

This has also given rise to projects of broader and more comprehensive scope. Many of our projects today comprise a number of different, but mutually supporting, components. It is obviously useful, for example, to base vocational training projects on a knowledge of a country's future manpower requirements, and there are many projects which combine these two components. Several of our management development projects also include assistance in such fields as personnel management, labor-management relations, and occupational safety and health, in view of the influence which all these matters can have on productivity. And, generally speaking, there has been an evident desire on the part of many countries to coordinate more fully the assistance they receive in different fields from the I.L.O.

The same considerations hold true for the assistance provided by other members of the United Nations family. There is a growing tendency, which I expect will become more pronounced in the future, for the I.L.O. to operate projects jointly with other organizations. As examples of such cooperation, I would cite the Rural Development Program in Congo (Brazzaville) which is being carried out in association with the F.A.O. and U.N.E.S.C.O.; the Institute of Small Industries in Giza, United Arab Republic, carried out by the I.L.O. in association with the United Nations Industrial Development Organization (U.N.I.D.O.); and the Institute for Training and Research in Agrarian Reform in Chile, carried out by the F.A.O. in association with the I.L.O.

But the key to the proper planning, coordination,

implementation, and follow-up of technical cooperation projects lies, and has always lain, with the governments of the beneficiary countries themselves. They are, as it were, the senior partners in this operation; international organizations like the I.L.O. can do no more than give the best advice and assistance available.

Evolution of Standard Setting

The new emphasis on operational work has not meant that the I.L.O. has neglected or lost sight of the more traditional area of its work—the elaboration of international labor standards. Quite the contrary. The standard-setting activities of the I.L.O. have remained a vital part of its work. Nevertheless, during the last twenty years the standard-setting work of the I.L.O. has necessarily undergone significant changes.

On the one hand, the number of new Conventions has declined. The first 31 sessions of the Conference until 1948 adopted a total of 90 Conventions, approximately three per session. Since 1949 the 21 sessions have adopted 38 Conventions, approximately two per session. Thus, on an average, the Conference has recently been adopting only two-thirds as many Conventions as previously.

But more important than the number of instruments adopted are the changes that have taken place

President Kennedy and Director-General Morse at a White House Meeting,
October 1963

An I.L.O. Rural Development Program in Chad

Left, The I.L.O. Headquarters on Lake Geneva, with the offices of the United Nations in the background

Right, The I.L.O. International Training Center at Turin

over the years in the aims and the content of these instruments. In the early years of the I.L.O.'s history, the primary aim of its standard-setting activities was to counteract what were considered to be the adverse effects of international economic competition on the conditions of working people, and to prevent certain countries from gaining unfair advantages in international trade by substandard labor laws and practices. More recently, it has been recognized that the relationship between labor standards and a country's competitiveness on the world market is not as clearcut as had at one time been thought. But this has not diminished the importance of international labor standards as instruments for international cooperation to achieve social progress. These standards, which set targets for national action, and which are adopted by the Conference representing the whole of the I.L.O.'s membership, serve as a stimulus to, and as a yardstick for, progress toward better and more humane working and living conditions.

The most important standards adopted by the I.L.O. during this period have been those relating to certain human rights.

All governments, on joining the Organization, have pledged their support for the broad principles of the I.L.O. Constitution—principles which are vital to the advancement of human dignity and to the effectiveness of the I.L.O.'s activities. The importance of these principles has been underlined since the Second World War through the adoption by the Conference of five international labor Conventions, which define in practical terms the essential features of national law or practice required in order to give effect to the principles. The five Conventions relate to freedom of association, the right to organize and to bargain collectively, the abolition of forced labor, the elimination of discrimination in employment, and equal pay for work of equal value. It is interesting and also encouraging to note that on the average these five Conventions, together with another two concerning freedom of association and forced labor which were adopted before the war, are among those that have been ratified by the largest number of member States.

The attention paid by the I.L.O. to the human rights which most closely affect the conditions of labor has influenced its postwar activities in various ways. The application of certain of these rights presents particular difficulties in countries at lower levels of development and this has given rise to a certain amount of controversy. There have been questions, for example, as to whether the policy of some developing countries to mobilize their human resources for development is not contrary to the I.L.O.'s forced labor standards. Consequently, in recent years, the I.L.O. has been concerned with helping developing countries find ways to achieve their development goals without excessive human cost. Another effect of the renewed attention paid to fundamental human rights within the Organization has been the establishment of new fact-finding machinery which has provided us with a growing fund of knowledge of the practical difficulties that arise in the application of the principles in question under different political, economic, and social conditions. In the field of freedom of association, special machinery has been built up, within the Governing Body in particular, to examine complaints alleging violation of trade union rights in certain countries.

Our aim has not been to condemn countries where these rights have not been effectively enjoyed. We have, above all, been attempting to offer our member States practical guidance on ways in which obstacles to the full application of human rights can be overcome.

Apart from the adoption of these human rights standards and of special machinery to ensure their application, there have been two important trends in the I.L.O.'s standard setting over the past twenty years.

First, steps have been taken to provide greater flexibility in the requirements of the Conventions. These measures have included the insertion in the Conventions of optional parts or alternative parts, the setting of more flexible standards for certain countries, and provision for certain exceptions, for example in regard to sparsely populated areas.

Second, the need for greater flexibility has led to the revision and updating of older Conventions, either to take account of changes in economic or social conditions, or to facilitate their ratification and application.

As a result of the movement toward greater flexibility, there has been a tendency for a large number of international labor standards to take the less rigid form of the Recommendation. Recommendations, which may be accepted in whole or in part, are particularly suitable for meeting the varied needs of countries in widely differing stages of economic and social development; often they spell out in some detail the ways in which the objectives of an accompanying Convention can be attained by countries at various levels of development.

I would like to emphasize that the adoption by the Conference of Conventions and Recommendations is merely the first stage in a lengthy process. The practical value of international standards depends on their application in the law and practice of the member countries. It is, of course, for each member country to decide for itself whether it can apply this or that international standard. But there is much that the I.L.O. can do to assist. In recent years there has been a marked improvement in this respect. The machinery for the mutual supervision of the application of Conventions and Recommendations has been remodelled. As a result, governments now report much more fully on action taken to apply Conventions they have ratified and Recommendations they have accepted, and also on the state of their national law and practice in relation to certain basic international instruments.

Rationalization and Decentralization

The vast increase in the size and diversity of the I.L.O.'s membership and the change in emphasis in our work have made it necessary over the past twenty years to create and strengthen regional machinery and regional activities. In its early days the I.L.O., as an international organization, had laid stress on its over-all universal mission; while differences in the needs of particular countries were recognized, little was done to provide for special consideration of those needs on a regional basis. In 1936, a tentative beginning was made by convening the first regional I.L.O. Conference for its American States Members at Santiago de Chile. The success of that experiment eventually led, not only to subsequent American Conferences, but also to the first Asian Conference in 1947, the first European Conference in 1955, and the first African Conference in 1960. It is now customary for one regional conference to be held each year. And in the interval between regional conferences, regional advisory committees advise the Governing Body on the evolution of regional needs and problems. These regional bodies have proved to be very useful tools for keeping the I.L.O. in close touch with the problems and preoccupations of each region, and for following and guiding the I.L.O.'s activities in the regions.

This has been paralleled by a progressive strengthening of the field services of the Office. During the very early years of the Organizations existence, branch offices and national correspondents were established in certain of the I.L.O's member States to serve as a link between the I.L.O. and those States. With the launching of our operational programs in 1949, I felt the need for a new type of field office, which would be responsible for all the technical assistance activities in a given region, and would provide an instrument for the close and continuing collaboration, which I discussed earlier, between the I.L.O. and the countries receiving assistance. The first "field office" of this nature, staffed by international officials, was set up in Asia in 1949. And by the early 1960's there were two field offices in Latin America, two in Africa, one in Asia, and one in the Middle East.

During the past three years, I have been intensifying this process of decentralization. The network of offices in the field is being greatly strengthened. Field offices are now called "area offices," each covering a small number of countries. The area offices, in turn, are directed by a regional office in each region, under the direction of a Regional Coordinator who is responsible for all the I.L.O.'s programs and projects within the region. More and more of the I.L.O.'s technical staff are being posted out to the regions to provide governments with technical advice on the spot and to assist them in the preparation of technical cooperation projects.

The decentralization and regionalization of our activities will not, however, affect only technical cooperation. I am also gradually decentralizing to the field certain aspects of other functions, such as research, information, the application of standards, and general relations functions.

But I would make one thing clear: the intensification of our regional work does not mean any weakening of the I.L.O.'s world-wide mission. Quite the contrary. While increasingly important functions may devolve on the I.L.O.'s regional bodies and field structure, central policy control will always remain with the I.L.O.'s policy-making bodies: the Conference, the Governing Body, and the International Labor Office in Geneva. I view the strengthening of regional activities as a means of increasing the I.L.O.'s capacity to attain its world-wide objectives by bringing it closer to regional and national realities, rather than as a threat to the universal character of the Organization.

Individual Industry Approach

Throughout its existence, the I.L.O. has been concerned in various ways with the social and labor problems of particular industries and categories of workers. Since its inception, of course, the I.L.O. has been very concerned with the protection of seafarers, and the Joint Maritime Commission has been in existence since 1920. It was not, however, until 1945 that Industrial Committees came into being as standing tripartite organs for the consideration of conditions in particular industries or affecting special occupational groups.

The Industrial Committees were established to fill what was considered to be a most important gap in the structure and program of the Organization, namely, the absence of machinery through which the particular and practical needs and problems of the principal industries could receive detailed technical consideration by persons with direct knowledge and experience of such industries.

They were to be a means of bringing men together in the matters which affect them most directly, the conditions of their daily working life in their chosen occupations. In this way the Committees were to develop mutual understanding and fruitful cooperation between management and labor with a view to improving working and living conditions of the workers and at the same time promoting the dynamic prosperity of the world's great industries. It was also suggested that by concentrating on social and labor problems of a strictly technical nature concerning their own industries, while avoiding discussion of issues of a political nature outside their sphere, the Industrial Committees would be in a particularly advantageous position to create a climate of genuine international cooperation between countries of different economic systems and in different stages of development. Finally, it was understood that the Industrial Committees would confine themselves to considering labor problems primarily affecting their own particular industries and would not discuss broader issues more suitable for consideration by the International Labor Conference. They would attempt in their deliberations to work out guidelines for their respective industries based on a general and broad consensus rather than on a majority vote on controversial issues.

What then has been accomplished by these Industrial Committees? Some eighty sessions of Industrial Committees covering the major world industries or occupational groups have been held since 1945. They have kept the I.L.O. in contact with the realities of different industries; and they have provided a unique forum in which the representatives of governments, workers, and employers principally affected by the world's major industries have exchanged experiences and thus participated in the work of international cooperation. Participation in tripartite Industrial Committee meetings has in itself been of great educational value for delegates concerned with the improvement of labor-management relations in their respective industries.

In the course of the years the different Industrial Committees have served as a forum for examining in the specific context of their industry such fundamental social problems as vocational training, conditions of work, and labor-management relations. In addition, their continuing vitality is illustrated by the fact that some of the most serious new social problems in today's world have been first examined at the international level by Industrial Committees. Thus, it was in the Metal Trades Committee in 1957 that the social effects of automation were discussed for the first time, I believe, in an international organization. More recently, the Committees have turned their attention to such problems as the social consequences of structural changes occurring in the various industries—some in the ascent, others in decline—and of the industrialization process in developing countries, the social and labor aspects of changes in international trade, and the trend of international concentration in some industries. The Committees are in this way doing a kind of pioneer work for the I.L.O. as a whole, keeping constantly abreast of the newest developments and realities of our industrial world, in respect not only of the newly industrializing nations but also of the traditionally industrial countries.

The guidelines worked out by the Industrial Committees have, in a great number of countries, demonstrably stimulated action by governments, industry, and trade unions for the improvement of conditions in individual industries, and have influenced collective bargaining in various countries. And they have given decisive impetus to some outstanding achievements, such as the Agreements among the riparian countries of the Rhine, concerning the conditions of employment and social security of Rhine boatmen; the Individual Control Book for Drivers in Road Transport, which is now incorporated in some national legislation and has also been included in a regional agreement on road transport worked out by the United Nations; and the Minimum Age (Underground Work) Convention (No. 123) 1965.[4] The list

---

[4]At its second session (1947), the Inland Transport Committee adopted a resolution *(Official Bulletin,* vol. 31, no. 2, September 15, 1948, p. 97) requesting the Governing Body to take steps with a view to the convocation of a special tripartite conference for the international regulation of social security and conditions of work in navigation on the Rhine. As a result, such a Conference was held in 1949. It "marked a new departure in the work of the I.L.O. in that it was concerned not merely with the definition of labour standards of general application but with the establishment of precise and detailed conditions for a clearly defined, limited body of workers" *(I/L/R,* vol. 61, no. 2, February 1950, p. 105). "Thus this Conference...may be described as the first step on the path foreshadowed in 1943. When the representative

of such examples could be extended, but the foregoing is sufficient to demonstrate the vitality and value of the Industrial Committees in the framework of the I.L.O.'s over-all activities.

Educational, Research, and Training Activities

I have long felt that the success of the I.L.O.'s work—in all its aspects—depends to a very large extent on the existence of trained, informed and responsible leadership in all countries and in all walks of life. Such leadership is needed in the factories, in the villages, and in government administrations. The I.L.O. has for many years aimed, particularly through its programs of workers' education, management development, and labor administration, to train people to work out and apply in their own ways solutions to the social problems of their communities, and thus to meet the growing need for popular participation in, and support for, the tasks of national development.

---

of the U.K. Government submitted to the G.B. the original proposal to establish the industrial committees, he argued that such committees might promote the negotiation of agreements of an international character no less effective than collective agreements made within the different countries" (*ibid.*, p. 117). The final texts of the general provisions of the two agreements concerning conditions of employment and social security, respectively, were adopted at a conference of governments held in Paris in July 1950. (*Fifth Report of the International Labour Organisation to the United Nations*, p. 117).

Nevertheless, I felt that there was a very serious gap in all our activities. I felt that the I.L.O. needed to bring together the leaders of tomorrow's society from different parts of the world and expose them to intensive education on the major social and economic problems of the world in which they would shortly be playing a leading role. It was these considerations that led me to propose to the Conference and Governing Body in 1959 the creation of an International Institute for Labor Studies. The Institute was established in 1960 and has been operational since 1962.

In its first few years, it concentrated exclusively on educational work. Some forty participants at a time from all over the world attended intensive three-month courses on various aspects of economic and social policy. These courses continue to be held, with very valuable results. But it has become clear that an international institute cannot by itself hope to meet this need for training leaders informed in rational methods of policy making. In addition, therefore, the Institute now conceives its role as encouraging and assisting university centers in developing areas to provide this type of educational service locally. The Institute in Geneva has become, as it were, an educational laboratory developing new methods and programs of leadership education so that these improved programs can be put to work in national educational centers where they reach larger numbers of people.

The Institute is also undertaking research which

complements that of the I.L.O. and fills somewhat different needs. It is concerned with long-term trends in society whereas the I.L.O.'s research is more action-oriented. As a result of the freedom of initiative which the Institute has in research, and of the fact that individual authors rather than institutions are responsible for the views expressed, the Institute is becoming a university-like institution and, therefore, a very valuable organ of the I.L.O. It also serves as a link between the academic community and the I.L.O. and is the world intellectual center concerned with development of social policy. The Institute took the lead in establishing in 1966 the International Industrial Relations Association, which links national associations of industrial relations specialists in most of the highly industrialized countries of the world and encourages the formation of such associations for other countries. The Institute has served as secretariat for the Association since its inception.

Another institution recently set up under I.L.O. auspices is the International Center for Advanced Technical and Vocational Training in Turin. Opened at the end of 1965, with the cooperation of the Italian Government, the Center provides advanced training in a wide variety of fields of management and vocational training. In its initial experimental period, the Center addressed itself primarily to meeting needs for training in developing countries. Participants from 102 countries have attended courses in workshops, laboratories, seminar rooms, and lecture halls; in-plant training in 23 industrialized countries has been arranged for participants in the programs. A recently completed evaluation survey indicates that participants returning to their home countries have in general successfully applied in their former working environment the knowledge and skills acquired in the Center.

The program for the operation of the Center during the next four-year period (1969–1972), as approved by the Board of the Center early this year, provides that, while advanced training of vocational and technical instructors will continue in a wide range of engineering fields, particular emphasis will be placed on management training, with courses on specific aspects of management of particular types of enterprises, including cooperatives.

In this field of management, moreover, many advanced countries are still finding their way. European countries from East and West alike are definitely interested in learning the most modern management techniques which have been developed in particular in the United States. The Turin Center is therefore arranging for an exchange of views between managers and professors of management from the industrial areas of the world as well as from the developing regions. In my capacity as Chairman of the Board of the Center I am glad to take this opportunity of expressing my gratification that an agreement had been reached between the Center and the School of Industrial and Labor Relations at this University for the establishment of a far-reaching joint program which will permit American professors to participate fully in this experiment, as well as in the other activities of the Center, which is now fully equipped to make its services available to an increasing number of participants.

So far, in the first three years of operation of the Center, the number of participants has averaged 500 a year; the goal to be attained by 1970 has been set at a minimum of 1,500 fellows per year, receiving fellowships of an average duration of four months. When that number is reached, a real impact can be expected on the economic and social development of the participating countries.

The I.L.O. Today

During my 20 years as Director-General, I have seen the I.L.O. change in many ways. My colleagues and I have been searching for ways to make the I.L.O. a truly effective instrument for peace, progress, and social justice. New types of action have been undertaken and new tools devised for this task. We have passed through a number of crises and suffered many disappointments. But these were the growing pains of a rapidly growing organization. Now, I feel, we have passed the stage of growing pains. The growth of the Organization has in many ways been stabilized or, at least, has become less dramatic.

This was why, already in 1963, I felt that it was time to take stock of the I.L.O.'s position in the world and to consider how its programs, procedures, and methods of action could and should be adjusted to keep the Organization attuned to the needs and problems of the modern world. In my reports to the Conference in 1963, 1964, and 1965,[5] I made proposals to that effect. And a large-scale, comprehensive debate ensued, which has still not been completed.

What have been and will be the results of this debate? How does the I.L.O. stand at the end of the first fifty years of its existence? What are the major challenges which await it in the future? And how will the I.L.O. respond to these challenges?

I propose to examine these questions in my third lecture.

---

[5] *Report of the Director-General: Programme and Structure of the I.L.O."* Report I, International Labour Conference, 47th sess., Geneva, 1963 (Geneva, 1963); *Report of the Director-General: Programme and Structure of the I.L.O., with Guidelines for the Discussion in 1964,* International Labour Conference, 48th sess., Geneva, 1964 (Geneva, 1964); *Report of the Director-General,* Report I (Part I), International Labour Conference, 49th sess., (Geneva, 1965).

THIRD LECTURE

The Role of the I.L.O. in the World Community

IN MY two previous lectures I have tried to give you an idea of what the I.L.O. is, what it stands for, how it has developed. The picture I have been trying to paint in very broad strokes is of a tripartite organization with world-wide membership; a normative, educational, and operational organization; an organization which for fifty years has been attempting in different ways to promote world-wide respect for the freedom and dignity of the working man and to create the conditions in which that freedom and dignity can be more fully and effectively enjoyed.

I should at this point like to examine the question whether an organization of this nature still has a role to play in today's world and that of tomorrow. Has the I.L.O. outlived its usefulness? If not, what is its role to be? And to what extent does it need to adapt itself in order to play this role?

77

The whole of the I.L.O.'s membership has for the past few years been engaged in a searching and critical examination of the program and structure of the organization in order to answer these very questions. The debate will be continued, and perhaps concluded, at next year's session of the Conference.

It would be quite improper for me to prejudge the outcome of this debate, which is still uncertain. But already a number of conclusions have emerged which enable us to see more clearly where we should go from here, and what role the I.L.O. should play in the world today.

Economic and Social Progress through World Planning

For many years now, the organizations of the United Nations system have been concentrating their efforts on the problems of the developing countries of the world. Each in its own sphere has been experimenting with new approaches, devising new methods for filling the gap between income levels and living conditions of the rich and the poor nations.

In order to draw the attention of the world to the magnitude and the urgency of this task, the United Nations General Assembly decided that the 1960's should be declared the "United Nations Development Decade." For this Decade a number of fairly precise objectives were set to achieve higher levels of development, and each of the organizations in the United Nations system was given a role to play in their attainment. The I.L.O.'s role was to bring about better utilization of human resources through employment and training and to ensure fuller popular participation in the development process.

This Development Decade is now nearly at an end. And it is already clear that the goals which were set will not be attained.[1] Not only will they not be attained; in many areas of the world incomes and living standards will actually have declined compared with 1960.

It is not too early to begin drawing lessons from the experience of the Development Decade, and indeed various United Nations bodies are already doing so. There are certain obvious reasons, quite independent of international organizations, for the failure of the Development Decade to achieve its goals. The industrialized countries did not provide anything like the level of resources required, in spite of the fact that they nearly all reached high levels of economic growth. The developing countries, for their part, have not always used the assistance they received to the best advantage. In addition, even

---

[1]"...To attain in each under-developed country a substantial increase in the rate of growth,...taking as the objective a minimum annual rate of growth of aggregate national income of 5 percent at the end of the Decade." General Assembly Resolution 1710 (XVI).

79

where economic development was achieved in absolute terms, it was nullified in many countries by rapid population growth and deteriorating terms of trade.

But the organizations of the United Nations family themselves, including the I.L.O., must bear a fair share of the responsibility. For while we were able to set fairly precise targets for the Decade, and thereby to raise great expectations, we were not able to define, with anything like the same precision, the methods by which these goals were to be achieved. Moreover, each organization tended to pursue its activities more or less independently of the others or, at least, with insufficient coordination.

That is why the whole United Nations system is beginning to look beyond the present Development Decade and to draw the necessary conclusions from the relatively discouraging record of achievement. And as I understand it, the most significant conclusion we are drawing is that, if the United Nations system is not to become discredited as an instrument for economic and social development, it must approach its task in a more rational, more closely coordinated, and above all more carefully *planned* manner. And if it is to obtain the resources needed to have an impact on the problem, it must show that it can use the resources which are made available to it in the most efficient way.

This means that we must set targets that are realistic, based on a careful assessment of what is possible and practical. We must plan our activities—all our activities—in relation to these targets. We must measure what we have achieved at each stage against what we set out to achieve. And we must be prepared to adjust our action accordingly. This, in turn, means that the different organizations of the United Nations system must work together in closer harmony than has been the case in the past.

This is the challenge that faces the I.L.O., as well as all other United Nations agencies, in the years that lie ahead.

Until recently, the I.L.O. and its member States have tended to adopt a piecemeal approach to social problems. Measures for vocational training have, for example, not always been coordinated with employment targets; incomes policies and social security schemes have rarely been devised in conjunction with other measures and objectives of economic and social policy.

But social policy needs to be considered as a whole complex of practical, interrelated measures carefully designed so as to make a positive and lasting contribution to the achievement of the fundamental goals which a society has set for itself, such as freedom from want, social and economic progress, and equality of opportunity. Such a social policy would be self-defeating, however, if it did not take economic realities fully into account, for it could not then make a lasting impact on the problem of poverty. It must be based on a careful evaluation of the comparative cost and anticipated benefits of each measure. It must not seek development at excessive human cost, and it must remain steadfastly oriented toward the fundamental social goals, as I have mentioned.

Such an approach to social policy needs, however, to be based on a number of clearly defined priorities, since there will always be a limit to the resources available for social purposes. And although the priorities fixed by different countries may vary, priorities must also be fixed on a world-wide level for the work of the I.L.O. and these must be based on a careful assessment of the urgency of the problems with which the I.L.O. has to deal.

There are, of course, limits on the extent to which the I.L.O. can fix firm priorities. In the view of some people, the I.L.O. is primarily a standard-setting organization whose most important task is to defend the rights of workers and to protect them from exploitation in the drive for growth, development, and industrialization. In the view of others, the I.L.O. is fundamentally an operational organization which needs to concentrate its efforts on promoting the economic development of the proper countries. Certain people see the I.L.O.'s main value as a forum for tripartite discussion; others see it as an organization providing assistance in the training of the labor force.

The truth is that the actual situation of the I.L.O. contains elements of each of these positions, And it is necessary that this be so if the I.L.O. is to continue to command the respect and support of all its constituents.

The first step in this process of determination of the I.L.O.'s priorities was the discussion in the Conference and subsequently in the Governing Body, beginning in 1963, of the program and structure of the I.L.O. There has been and continues to be a certain amount of disagreement on the structure of the Organization, particularly with respect to the distribution of powers and responsibilities between the Conference and the Governing Body, and the composition of the latter—although even in these respects long and patient negotiation and compromise are beginning to bear fruit. But with respect to matters of program a very substantial measure of agreement was reached.

As a result of this debate, it was decided to group all the I.L.O.'s activities under three major comprehensive programs: human resources, social institutions development, and conditions of work and life. Departments corresponding to each of these major programs were then established in the Office.

The next step is to define the objectives of these major programs, and to determine priorities within and between them. This will be a long and difficult task, because to establish priorities means to redirect resources from one field of I.L.O. action to another; and since many of the I.L.O.'s activities have their own "constituency" there will inevitably be sharp differences of opinion as to which program should be emphasized and which should be de-emphasized or even phased out completely.

Another basic problem is that, once the program objectives are defined, it will be necessary to determine which method of action or combination of methods of action can best contribute to the attainment of these objectives—standard-setting, meetings of experts, regional action, technical cooperation, research, Industrial Committee meetings, and so on. Here, the problem is that the I.L.O.'s constituents sometimes regard each of these methods of action as ends in themselves. Certain people claim, for example, that the I.L.O. has adopted enough Conventions and Recommendations, and that the aim should now be to ensure the application of existing instruments; others feel that this is the most important aspect of the I.L.O.'s work and should be continued with undiminished vigor. But few ask whether the adoption of a Convention or a Recommendation will serve to advance the attainment of a specific objective in a given field better than any other form of action.

We have now installed in the Office a system of program planning—in which the Conference and the

Governing Body are associated—which aims to plan the I.L.O.'s activities in both the short and the long term in relation to clearly defined objectives. Although the new system of programing has not yet been able to resolve fully the problems to which I have just referred, this will certainly come in time. And, in my view, this approach is essential if the I.L.O. is to find a new sense of purpose in the world today.

World Employment Program

There is one priority in the I.L.O.'s present and future programs which is clearly recognized as being paramount—namely, a program for employment and training which is to be known as the World Employment Program. This program is to be officially launched next year; its launching will highlight our 50th anniversary year.

As I indicated in Lecture II, the I.L.O. has for many years been concerned with the training of workers of different categories and levels. In terms of expenditure this has long been the most important of all the I.L.O.'s activities. As I also pointed out, employment questions have long been an important concern of the I.L.O. Guidelines for national and international action to raise levels of productive employment were laid down in a Convention and Recommendation on Employment Policy adopted by the

Conference in 1964. The World Employment Program, however, is an entirely new departure for the I.L.O.

It may be useful to analyze the reasons why this program is of such high priority for the I.L.O. In my view, the problem of unemployment and underemployment in the developing countries has reached such serious proportions that it must be given priority attention in any strategy for economic and social development. In fact, even where economic development has been successful, judged by such criteria as increase in gross national product, it has generally failed to resolve the problem of creating productive employment to keep pace with the increasing labor force. For this reason, large sectors of the populations of developing countries have been bypassed by the economic progress that has been achieved.

Moreover, because of the population explosion, these problems are certain to become even more serious in the next two decades; opportunities for work have not increased in the past at the same rate as the population of working age, and will not do so in the future unless concerted action is taken. Rural populations, in particular, while not unemployed in the sense that they have no work to do, often work only during a very small part of their time, with primitive methods and at very low levels of productivity. It is not surprising, therefore, that living standards are appallingly low.

Parallel to this there is the equally serious problem of the unemployed in the large cities of the world—and particularly in the developing world, where job opportunities are scarce and where low levels of training and education make it difficult for the unemployed to find work in industry.

This situation represents a serious obstacle to development since it means a waste of human resources and thus an underutilization of a nation's productive forces; the low and declining levels, or indeed the almost total lack of income which results from unemployment and underemployment, are causing growing frustration and discontent among vast sections of the world's population; and this constitutes a serious and growing threat to world peace.

In short, the I.L.O.—and indeed the whole of the United Nations family—can make no headway in all their other tasks unless some progress is made in eliminating this basic cause of poverty and underemployment. That is the ambitious objective of the World Employment Program. And that is why it is being given the highest priority in the I.L.O's activities.

For it is now recognized that employment levels can only be raised and existing employment made more productive through a conscious effort and through a deliberate policy. In the past it was assumed that higher levels of productive employment would be created automatically as a result of economic development. Experience has proved this assumption to be false, particularly as the world's population has grown faster than most demographers predicted. The I.L.O. assumed that, by assisting in the training of large numbers of people, it would make it possible to raise levels of employment. We now realize that our activities for training need to form part of a dynamic employment policy.

The increasing concern of member States about problems of unemployment, underemployment, and manpower planning has been reflected in recent meetings of our regional advisory committees and regional conferences. These included proposals and plans adopted at the Regional Conference of American States in 1966 and in particular at the Asian Regional Conference in Tokyo last month. And at the request of the African Advisory Committee, the Office will place a draft "Jobs and Skills Program" for Africa before the African Regional Conference to be held next year.

The World Employment Program will, therefore, be composed of the regional manpower plans adopted by the I.L.O.'s regional bodies. For each region and subregion of the world—or at least of the developing world—we shall make recommendations as to how productive employment can be increased within a given time period, through appropriate training, rural development, small-scale industry development, youth employment schemes, and other policies.

We shall then give our member States in each of these regions whatever assistance they may request to meet these needs. And progress will be kept under continuing review by our regional conferences and advisory committees, as well as by the Governing Body, so that we can see how our action may be improved, intensified, or adjusted to reach the targets set.

The World Employment Program will, therefore, represent a first attempt at truly world-wide planning in one important area of our work, namely, the field of human resources development.

Our aim is to coordinate and associate our efforts in these activities with those of other United Nations agencies and regional bodies, as well as bilateral programs for development assistance; these organizations are already working with us in setting up the World Employment Program.

For employment depends on many factors beyond the I.L.O's control. It depends on the pace of economic growth, on investment policies, on the relative weight given to the development of industry and agriculture, on educational policies, and on many other factors. For this reason, the World Employment Program will represent a joint effort by many organizations, under the leadership of the I.L.O.

Moreover, I hope that, as the I.L.O.'s World Employment Program develops, it and similar long-term plans by other agencies, such as the F.A.O.'s Indicative World Plan for Agricultural Development and U.N.E.S.C.O.'s World Literacy Campaign, will become integral parts of a world-wide plan for over-all economic development which is now being elaborated by the United Nations.

In this way the United Nations family of organizations will become a more powerful force for planned development. It will become a real, united family working harmoniously toward very precise, realistic, and mutually supporting objectives instead of more or less vague and very far-off goals. And through the World Employment Program, the I.L.O. will have an important and positive role to play in this process.

This new approach to development will also, I hope, result in a new approach to interagency relations. In the past, the various organizations of the United Nations system have, in my view, all too often been engaged in sterile and unproductive controversies concerning demarcations of competence. While it remains essential that there should be as little overlapping as possible in the activities of the different organizations, it is inevitable that there will be certain "grey areas" where the interests and activities of two or more organizations overlap—a problem, moreover, that is not unknown among government departments. It is by undertaking joint action in areas where a strict demarcation of responsibilities is difficult or impossible, rather than by endless disputes over which organization should have responsibility for what, that this problem can best be overcome. This is a pragmatic, functional approach that we are attempting to implement in the World Employment Program; and this is the approach which my colleagues, the Directors-General of F.A.O. and U.N.E.S.C.O., and I have recently agreed upon in the field of agricultural education in which we all have common interests.

I have mentioned the World Employment Program first because it represents such an important priority in the I.L.O.'s action, and because it signifies for the I.L.O. a radically new approach to its task. But it is by no means the only field in which the I.L.O. has an important role to play in the modern world. I should therefore like to mention briefly the types of problems with which the I.L.O. will have to come to grips in our other major programs—in the development of social institutions and in the improvement of conditions of work and life.

Development of Social Institutions

The rapid and revolutionary process of change through which the world is now passing is bringing about new types of social relationships and creating new areas of social and political conflict. As a result—in both advanced and developing countries—the traditional institutions for regulating human relations and for organizing the life of society are proving to be inadequate and ill-adapted to the needs of the modern world. Yet attempts to devise new institutional arrangements have failed to keep pace with the process of economic and technological change. As a result, we are witnessing today a wave of unrest throughout the world—particularly among young people—which aims at remaking or replacing existing forms of social and political organizations in such a way as to permit those who consider themselves inadequately represented or unrepresented to participate more directly in the life of their society.

The I.L.O. has long been concerned with the need for each society to develop and perfect institutions which offer the opportunity of participating in the vital social, economic, and political decisions of that society to each individual who is interested in so doing. Naturally, in its efforts to deal with problems in this area the I.L.O. must take account of the fact that the problems encountered in the developing countries differ markedly from those in the industrialized countries.

The work of the I.L.O. takes the form, in the developing countries, of assisting in building up those institutions and forms of social organization which are essential for the transition to a modern economy and society. In this connection, we attach great importance to the development of sound systems of industrial relations through which it is possible for the State and representatives of employers and workers to engage in a process of dialogue and accommodation. Yet we are faced here with a number of very difficult and controversial problems.

Trade unions are often weak and poorly organized in developing countries; yet how can they be strengthened and supported by governments without being unduly influenced and even dominated by them? When trade unions are weak, how can employers be persuaded to negotiate and discuss with them or to adopt constructive personnel and labor relations policies without being accused of either exploitation or paternalism? How can there be meaningful collective bargaining? On the other hand, if trade unions in developing countries are strong and free, is there not a danger that they will prove to be an obstacle to development; that they may push up wages to a level that compromises national policies for investment and development; and that they may undermine national unity?

These problems illustrate the difficulties with which developing countries are faced in this field. And it is clear that the pattern of labor relations in developing countries cannot simply be modelled on that which has grown up in the industrialized countries of the West. The State will certainly have an important role to play in regulating working conditions and in settling industrial disputes. And trade unions, if they are to avoid undue interference from governments, will have to be quite as concerned with national interests as with the interests of their own members; they will have to act in a most responsible manner if they are to preserve their independence. The I.L.O. has, therefore, to give these countries assistance which takes full account of the difficult situations in which they find themselves, but which at the same time does not conflict with the I.L.O.'s basic principles of freedom of association. And so we are tackling the problem on several fronts at once.

We are helping trade unions in the training of their leaders.

We are assisting governments in strengthening their labor ministries, which have a key role to play in economic and social development.

We are advising governments in the drafting of labor legislation and in devising appropriate policies for regulating labor-management relations.

We are assisting employers on personnel management questions.

We are seeking to develop appropriate institutions which will permit a fuller integration of rural workers and rural populations into the life of a modern society which will otherwise pass them by.

We are helping to build up cooperatives and other institutions which can help rural workers—who constitute by far the largest part of the labor force—in improving their methods of production and in raising their standards of living.

And we are experimenting continually with new

ifferentials should be sufficient to provide workers with incentives to qualify for more highly skilled work and to increase productivity.

The I.L.O. is not concerned solely with assisting governments in fixing wage and income policies which meet all these requirements, although it does give such assistance when requested. The essential concern of the I.L.O. is that the methods used in devising income policies—whether it be through collective bargaining or through legislation or by any other means—be socially just and economically responsible; and that wherever possible employers and trade unions be participants in the formulation of such policies.

The I.L.O. is concerned with all other aspects of working conditions—hours of work, holidays with pay, occupational safety and health, and welfare and recreational facilities. And although the developing countries must for some time to come claim priority in the allocation of the I.L.O.'s resources in these fields, we cannot afford to overlook the problems faced by industrialized countries. Automation and technological change are presenting new and challenging problems of job and income security in these countries. Moreover, they are already beginning to result in increased leisure time for workers, thus calling for a greater availability of cultural and recreational facilities. All of this calls for new types of

approaches, new methods of action, to enable all sections of the population to participate in and to influence the course of the economic and social development of their country.

In the industrialized countries, the problem is rather one of adapting existing institutions and systems to meet the needs of technological and structural change.

In Eastern Europe experiments are being made with new forms of organizing production and with new systems which give the managers of undertakings greater responsibility and initiative. This may well lead to new types of relationships between managers and trade unions, and possibly to new methods of fixing conditions of employment.

In the industrialized countries of the West, on the contrary, there is a clear tendency for governments to intervene in fields which were previously regarded as the almost exclusive domain of trade unions and employers—in particular in the field of wage and price fixing—while at the same time to associate trade unions and employers' organizations in the formulation of national economic and social policy.

The I.L.O. is following these developments carefully; the various issues involved are subjects of research and tripartite discussion within the I.L.O. For there should be no mistaking the importance of the social changes that are sweeping through the world. And the I.L.O. must do its part to see that these changes are channelled in constructive directions and that the freedom and the material well-being of the working man are enhanced rather than impaired in this process of change.

Conditions of Work and Life

It has always been the fundamental purpose of the I.L.O. to improve the working and living conditions of workers everywhere. If I mention this broad area of I.L.O. concern last, it is not because the I.L.O. is, as it were, forgetting the basic reason for its existence. On the contrary, all the I.L.O.'s work under the World Employment Program and under the development of social institutions is aimed at creating the conditions in which the quality and standards of life of all people can be improved.

If, however, people are to be convinced of the usefulness of economic development, there must be quite prompt improvement in their conditions of life and work. Government plans and programs are beginning to be clearer on the point that the ultimate objective of economic development is social improvement. The I.L.O. has assisted the governments of developing countries in devising and applying social policies which meet the requirement of prompt and tangible effect and which seek to provide the worker with the maximum amount of protection in a given economic and social context.

Most of the wage-earning employme the modern sector of the economy is i and workers who leave the countrysi such employment have to face the p some day old age, sickness, or accider them and their dependents of their they may not be able to rely on the tra ance of the community from which t help guarantee the income of worker tate their commitment to their new v I.L.O. has helped governments to e security schemes, or pension funds, w additional advantage of accumulating ment.

Similarly, the I.L.O. is attempting ernments on the income policies wl appropriate in conditions of underdev the problem of striking a balance be socially just and what is economicall complex and delicate one. On the on and other income must be adequate t worker with at least sufficient resourc elementary needs: on the other hand, be so high as to jeopardize the attain economic and social goals, such as hi employment and greater access to w Likewise, it is necessary to do away wi equalities in income levels through measures of income distribution, an approaches, new methods of action, to enable all sections of the population to participate in and to influence the course of the economic and social development of their country.

In the industrialized countries, the problem is rather one of adapting existing institutions and systems to meet the needs of technological and structural change.

In Eastern Europe experiments are being made with new forms of organizing production and with new systems which give the managers of undertakings greater responsibility and initiative. This may well lead to new types of relationships between managers and trade unions, and possibly to new methods of fixing conditions of employment.

In the industrialized countries of the West, on the contrary, there is a clear tendency for governments to intervene in fields which were previously regarded as the almost exclusive domain of trade unions and employers—in particular in the field of wage and price fixing—while at the same time to associate trade unions and employers' organizations in the formulation of national economic and social policy.

The I.L.O. is following these developments carefully; the various issues involved are subjects of research and tripartite discussion within the I.L.O. For there should be no mistaking the importance of the social changes that are sweeping through the world. And the I.L.O. must do its part to see that these changes are channelled in constructive directions and that the freedom and the material well-being of the working man are enhanced rather than impaired in this process of change.

Conditions of Work and Life

It has always been the fundamental purpose of the I.L.O. to improve the working and living conditions of workers everywhere. If I mention this broad area of I.L.O. concern last, it is not because the I.L.O. is, as it were, forgetting the basic reason for its existence. On the contrary, all the I.L.O.'s work under the World Employment Program and under the development of social institutions is aimed at creating the conditions in which the quality and standards of life of all people can be improved.

If, however, people are to be convinced of the usefulness of economic development, there must be quite prompt improvement in their conditions of life and work. Government plans and programs are beginning to be clearer on the point that the ultimate objective of economic development is social improvement. The I.L.O. has assisted the governments of developing countries in devising and applying social policies which meet the requirement of prompt and tangible effect and which seek to provide the worker with the maximum amount of protection in a given economic and social context.

Role in the World Community

Most of the wage-earning employment available in the modern sector of the economy is in urban areas, and workers who leave the countryside to take up such employment have to face the possibility that some day old age, sickness, or accident may deprive them and their dependents of their livelihood and they may not be able to rely on the traditional assistance of the community from which they came. To help guarantee the income of workers and to facilitate their commitment to their new way of life, the I.L.O. has helped governments to establish social security schemes, or pension funds, which offer the additional advantage of accumulating capital investment.

Similarly, the I.L.O. is attempting to advise governments on the income policies which are most appropriate in conditions of underdevelopment. But the problem of striking a balance between what is socially just and what is economically possible is a complex and delicate one. On the one hand, wages and other income must be adequate to provide the worker with at least sufficient resources to meet his elementary needs: on the other hand, they must not be so high as to jeopardize the attainment of other economic and social goals, such as higher levels of employment and greater access to world markets. Likewise, it is necessary to do away with glaring inequalities in income levels through appropriate measures of income distribution, and yet income differentials should be sufficient to provide workers with incentives to qualify for more highly skilled work and to increase productivity.

The I.L.O. is not concerned solely with assisting governments in fixing wage and income policies which meet all these requirements, although it does give such assistance when requested. The essential concern of the I.L.O. is that the methods used in devising income policies—whether it be through collective bargaining or through legislation or by any other means—be socially just and economically responsible; and that wherever possible employers and trade unions be participants in the formulation of such policies.

The I.L.O. is concerned with all other aspects of working conditions—hours of work, holidays with pay, occupational safety and health, and welfare and recreational facilities. And although the developing countries must for some time to come claim priority in the allocation of the I.L.O.'s resources in these fields, we cannot afford to overlook the problems faced by industrialized countries. Automation and technological change are presenting new and challenging problems of job and income security in these countries. Moreover, they are already beginning to result in increased leisure time for workers, thus calling for a greater availability of cultural and recreational facilities. All of this calls for new types of action, even new functions, to be undertaken by governments, by trade unions, and by employers.

The I.L.O.'s aim is not, in short, simply to protect workers from exploitation and injury. It is also to demonstrate the salutary effects that good, safe, and humane working conditions can have on the workers' morale, and thus on the output and growth of the economy. We are passing from the *protection* of the worker to the *promotion* of a world-wide awareness of the importance—in both economic and social terms, in both developed and developing countries—of treating the worker as a human being, of devising measures to meet his material and spiritual needs, and of respecting his human rights.

Human Rights

The protection of human rights has figured prominently in the I.L.O.'s action, as I noted in my second lecture. One reason for this is that the goal of fuller recognition of human rights is as important as the satisfaction of material needs. Indeed, the two are inseparable. Human rights are empty to those who lack the material means of enjoying them. The pursuit of material well-being is meaningless unless it is accompanied by the opportunity for the free development of the individual personality, and by the spiritual development of the individual and of society as a whole.

The I.L.O. has always been aware of the importance of this principle. Yesterday I mentioned the important standards that have been adopted by the I.L.O. over the past twenty years in the field of basic human rights and freedoms. All the activities the I.L.O. is undertaking today and will be undertaking in the future are directed at ensuring the fuller enjoyment of these rights.

The World Employment Program is aimed at making a reality of the right to work, of freedom from forced labor, of equality of opportunity in employment. The I.L.O. activities for the development of social institutions are centered on the principle of freedom of association and aim to give substance to that principle. By improving conditions of work and life, we aim to promote the concept of the dignity of the human being.

We shall, of course, continue to strengthen our machinery for supervising the implementation of the I.L.O.'s standards on these questions. But to do no more than this would be irresponsible. We must at the same time do everything in our power to create the economic and material conditions in which this implementation can become possible. We have, therefore, to find a way around what some consider to be the apparent contradiction between human rights and economic development. We have to prove and establish that development is possible in conditions of freedom. More than that, we have to prove and establish that the freedom and dignity of the individual, and the freedom of the organizations to which he belongs, are, in the words of the Declaration of Philadelphia, actually "essential to sustained progress."

This is not an easy task. There is always the danger that individuals and organizations will use their freedom irresponsibly and selfishly; that they will undermine the efforts of society as a whole to achieve economic, social, cultural, and spiritual progress. That is why, as I mentioned yesterday, I attach so much importance to the educational aspects of the I.L.O.'s action, and why the International Institute of Labor Studies and the International Center for Advanced Technical and Vocational Training have such an important role to play in our work. For unless we can educate and train people not only for skills, but also for responsibilities; unless we can teach them to treasure and protect their own rights and freedoms, and to respect the rights, needs, and interests of others; unless we can teach them to learn from each other, to respect each other, rather than to be in constant conflict with each other; unless the I.L.O. can do these things, its work in all other fields, its attempts to promise human rights and freedoms, will surely fail.

Origin and Evolution of the I.L.O.

The I.L.O. and World Peace

I would like now to consider with you the I.L.O.'s role as an instrument for peace. The I.L.O. has since the end of the last war been a part of the United Nations system, linked to the United Nations by a formal agreement. It is thus fully committed to the fundamental objective of the United Nations, which is to preserve and strengthen the foundations of world peace. Hence it has a role to play, within the framework of the United Nations system, in the attainment of this objective.

The I.L.O. does not, of course, have any responsibility for peace-keeping and international security operations, which are the sole responsibility of the United Nations. Nor can it attempt to resolve political differences among States. What, then, has a body dealing with labor and social questions to do with peace?

I can best begin to answer this question by emphasizing that the I.L.O. forms part of a system of international law and international relations which has been gradually and painstakingly built up over the years. It provides an open forum for dialogue among very diverse political, social, and economic forces and interests. It provides the nations of the world with an instrument for collaboration rather than just confrontation, for cooperation rather than just hostility. If the I.L.O. ceased to exist, the world would lose a very useful instrument for peaceful cooperation; and the principle of the rule of law in international relations—which the I.L.O. has perhaps done more than any other organization to strengthen and promote—would be very seriously compromised. The world would also lose the most effective international tool yet devised to study and deal with the social and economic causes of unrest and with those elements of social disintegration which directly threaten world peace.

Furthermore, the I.L.O. makes it possible for the nations of the world to concentrate their attention on problems and issues which are common to them all, rather than just those which divide them. And by associating employers and workers in the process of international cooperation, the I.L.O. is able, to a greater extent than any other organization, to help instill this spirit of cooperation not only among diplomats but also among the representatives of the major economic and social forces of every nation.

In Lecture II, I referred to the difficulties experienced by the I.L.O. when certain countries of Eastern Europe entered or reentered the Organization in 1954. Some of these difficulties still persist, but by bringing together the employers and workers, as well as the governments of East and West, the I.L.O. has contributed in a significant manner to the world-wide effort to promote international understanding. Until the occurrence of the events in Czechoslovakia this summer, a movement toward cooperation between the trade unions of Eastern and Western Europe had gradually been developing, and this was very noticeably reflected in the forums of the I.L.O.

In addition, exchanges between the businessmen of the West and the managers of State-owned enterprises in the East had also been on the increase, and the Eastern European countries have been looking to the West, through the I.L.O., for assistance in implementing the advanced management techniques which have been developed in the West. It had been hoped that this trend represented a solid and significant development in the furthering of genuine international cooperation. But the question which remains unanswered as I speak to you this afternoon is what effect the events of this summer will have on this trend. Certainly, once again, the horizon looks stormy.[2]

In the "political" arena in which we work, the record of the International Labor Organization resembles a fever chart. Through the years, it has had high and low points of conflict or cooperation depending almost entirely on a force which is beyond the control of the Organization, namely, the inter-

---

[2]See the separate communiqués of the Brussels-based International Confederation of Free Trade Unions (August 21 and September 12, 1968) and International Federation of Christian Trade Unions (August 21, 1968), and the Prague-based World Federation of Trade Unions (August 28, 1968), each denouncing in its own terms and manner the invasion of Czechoslovakia.

national political climate. As I have just indicated, international organizations are today—at this very moment—once again being affected by the currents of political tension and controversy. There is the fear that the world may be returning to the days of the Cold War. My view is that, despite all of these difficulties and the stresses which are inherent in our work, international organizations must remain constant in their fidelity to the principles of objectivity and vigor in pursuing the goals of working for improved international understanding and for peace. After all, what are the alternatives? It seems to me that the most recent political crisis demonstrates that the search for areas of cooperation, mutual confidence, and the strengthening of international procedures for the protection and furthering of human rights must be intensified rather than weakened.

A key to the success of the I.L.O.'s contribution to this effort is the confidence that member states, and worker and employer representatives as well, have in the International Civil Service. It is essential that the honesty and objectivity of the international civil servant be in the forefront of our preoccupations, if the I.L.O. and the U.N. systems are to play their proper roles in what must continue to be an unceasing world-wide effort to safeguard peace and security. It is when the political climate is at its highest and most feverish temperature that we must try the hardest to promote the methods, procedures, and atmosphere to permit the peaceful resolution of issues; just as when the temperature cools we must struggle to gain every inch of ground and to strengthen the institutions and procedures for international cooperation so that the next crisis may hopefully be more readily controlled. It is only by such an approach, and philosophy, and faith in action, that we can hope effectively to contribute to the realization of the aims of the Constitution of the I.L.O. and the Charter of the United Nations.

The importance and value of this approach within the framework of the I.L.O.'s principles of tripartism and universality is highlighted by the fact that, while insisting upon these principles and upon the strengthening of the instrumentalities and procedures for collaboration, the International Labor Organization does not shrink from but encourages the confrontation and the testing of experiences and ideas which emerge from differing social and ideological concepts and backgrounds. It does not shrink from but encourages the constant testing of areas of freedom in human and industrial relations. It does not shrink from but encourages the testing of all issues of human rights, and of the broader issue of whether economic development can proceed in freedom, democratically, and with safeguards for the dignity of the individual.

Their tripartite structure permits the representative organs of the I.L.O. to deal effectively with complex and delicate problems. Employer and worker representatives, who generally act independently of the governments which nominate them, can articulate their views on these problems in a manner which the exigencies of protocol and considerations of possible diplomatic and political repercussions would not permit government representatives to do to the same extent. Thus, imaginative, responsible, and constructive suggestions for dealing with fundamental problems can be and are, in fact, placed before the forums of the I.L.O. by the employer and worker representatives, usually after consultations with other members of their respective groups, and are then fully debated. There have been numerous instances where this unique structure has permitted great obstacles to be overcome and new ground to be broken in the economic and social fields.

The I.L.O. is the one organization—perhaps because of its tripartite structure and its attachment to the principle of universality—where the concept of the "market place of ideas" is fully accepted and works. Looking back over fifty years of I.L.O. experience discloses something very important and often little understood by the public and even by those in academic life: that given such a "market place," and given its opportunity to function in an atmosphere where the I.L.O. constituents are confident that the rules of the game will be fairly and honestly applied and the procedures fully safeguarded, the outcome for the principles of social justice and freedom has never once been placed in doubt.

In the work of the I.L.O., the ideal of the dignity of the individual has never yet—not even once—been compromised or betrayed, but rather it has been strengthened. We see this in many ways: in our insistance upon "due process of law" in our approach to apartheid and the resultant effective condemnation of this policy; in our procedure for the handling of individual cases of alleged violation of freedom of association which has resulted in the release from detention or prison of large numbers of workers who had been detained or imprisoned because of legitimate trade union activity; in the acceptance by governments of changes in legislation in order to safeguard freedom of association; in our debates and inquiries and conventions on forced labor and their positive effects on national practices; in the debates on and development of our programs for the promotion of industrial relations and workers' education activities.

We also see this in our debates and programs dealing with discrimination in employment on the basis of race, color, sex, religion, political opinion, national extraction, or social origin, where attitudes on this question continue to be influenced and changed in a positive way. The I.L.O. Convention against discrimination has given those discriminated against the possibility of effective redress, through legal procedures or by rallying public opinion or both; discriminatory practices are openly disclosed and fully discussed and debated, and the experiences of various countries in dealing with this fundamental problem are examined and are constantly compared so that each country may benefit from the experiences of the others.

We also see this in our open fights and successes in eliminating child labor; in getting acceptance of the principle and practice of employment for the handicapped, of the concept of full employment, of the concept of equal pay for equal work, and so the list could go on and on.

I do not believe that the objectives of the United Nations system can ever be achieved by boycotting from membership or from participation those with whom there are ideological or other differences. This practice is necessarily counterproductive. The objectives of the U.N. system can only be achieved by the genuine acceptance of diversity and international pluralism—and the constant struggle of ideas and public opinion within the "market place" between widely divergent forces, until one day the universally proclaimed objectives of peace, security, freedom, and social justice may become a reality. This is a strategy for peace which in the long run must be accepted as the substitute for force and arms and violence if civilization is to survive. In this effort, the I.L.O., F.A.O., U.N.E.S.C.O., the World Bank, and all of the agencies of the U.N. have key roles to play. These are not isolated roles but must be seen as one, fully integrated within the political, economic, social, and financial framework of the total international effort for world peace, stability, and social justice. To weaken one link in this chain is to negate the entire effort. It is in this perspective that the work of the I.L.O. must be seen and appreciated.

A further way in which the I.L.O. influences and strengthens international cooperation is by offering opportunities for the channelling of development assistance from the industrialized nations to the developing countries. I have always been in complete agreement with the view of U Thant, Secretary-General of the United Nations, Paul Hoffman, Administrator of the United Nations Development Programme, and Robert McNamara, President of the World Bank who is the most recent arrival to the team of executive heads of international organizations, that the growing tensions and frustrations in the poverty-stricken nations represent a continuing serious danger and threat to peace.

That is why, as I stated earlier, by far the greatest part of the I.L.O.'s efforts and resources are being devoted to raising levels of living in the developing countries. For it is by pursuing its eminently practical, though perhaps undramatic, work in those countries that the I.L.O. is today making a most important contribution to peace. I believe that it is now at long last recognized by statesmen, educators, and leaders generally that higher standards of living and material welfare, as well as greater freedom, dignity, and justice among men, are essential elements in the achievement of peace.

In conclusion, I would come back to the question I asked at the beginning of this lecture. Does the I.L.O. still have a role to play? What can it do that nations, acting on their own, cannot achieve? I would sum up the answer I have attempted to give in these lectures in the following terms.

The most important guiding principle of the I.L.O. on which the whole of its action rests, and to which all of its member States subscribe, at least in theory, is that "poverty anywhere constitutes a danger to prosperity everywhere." This means that the nations of the world cannot afford to consider the social problems of any one country as being the exclusive concern of that country. In the I.L.O. they have an instrument to pool their resources and their expertise for a concerted world-wide attack on poverty; they have an opportunity to demonstrate by practical action the truth of the principle that the attack on poverty, wherever it exists, is the collective responsibility of the whole of mankind; and they can demonstrate that collective action is more effective than the sum total of the efforts of each country acting individually. The I.L.O., acting in concert with other organizations of the United Nations system, is therefore, above all, a living testimony to the ideal of the *solidarity* of mankind.

However admirable this principle may be in theory, it is not easy to translate into practice. There is always the danger that the nations of the world—employers and workers, as well as governments—will either sink into comfortable but short-sighted parochialism, or will be so obsessed with their own domestic problems that they will have little time to spare for the problems of others. This danger is probably at least as great now as it ever was. There is today a serious risk that the richer nations will lose genuine interest in the outside world, and that they will fail to see or to understand, or that they will underestimate, the new tensions that will inevitably arise from the growing frustrations of the poor and the underprivileged. Within this statement of position resides the most serious threat to the achievement of world peace and international stability. It is for the sum of these reasons that I believe that there is a greater need today than ever before for the I.L.O. to arouse the social conscience of mankind and to stimulate it to constructive and positive action.

At the same time, the I.L.O. itself is faced with a challenge. It needs resources—and far more resources than it has available today—to carry on its work. But if it is to obtain these resources, it has to prove to the world that it is an efficient and effective instrument in the attack on poverty; that it is, in other words, a good investment for peace and prosperity. It has to adjust its program and its methods of action to gain or to maintain the confidence of its members.

It must, at the same time, be aware of its own limitations. The I.L.O. is not a world-wide Ministry of Labor or Ministry of Social Affairs. It can set guidelines for national action, and stimulate such action, and assist in its implementation when requested. But it cannot substitute itself for governments, or for trade unions, or for employers' organizations.

In other words, the I.L.O. can only be as effective an instrument for progress as its member States and its other constituents want it to be. It will only have the resources that the nations of the world, and particularly the richer nations, are willing to give it. And it can have no more influence on national legislation and national practice than its member States want it to have.

Despite all of these difficulties and shortcomings, I believe that the I.L.O. contributes in a significant manner to long-term world peace. It may not have executive powers, but it exercises substantial influence over national policies. It enjoys considerable prestige in the world, because it stands for principles and for a progressive and essentially pragmatic approach to social policy that are recognized to have a universal validity. It provides the governments, employers, and workers of the world with a meeting

113

ground and with a framework for international dialogue. It is a school for *cooperation* where men and women of different backgrounds and different interests can learn to understand each other, to discover common problems and commonly held aspirations and principles, and to undertake joint and common action to promote the realization of these aspirations and principles.

The parallel development of the growing gap between the rich and the poor, and the shrinking of the globe by reason of modern means of communications and transportation, is placing the world in an increasingly dangerous and potentially explosive situation. At the same time, this situation offers greater scope and possibility of cooperation than ever before. That is why I am convinced that the I.L.O. has now and will continue to have a role in international affairs which is even more vital than its founding fathers envisaged when they gave the Organization its original mandate fifty years ago. However, if the I.L.O. is to continue to meet its original challenge and the challenge as we now see it for the years which lie ahead, it will be essential that the Organization continue to be alert to change and continue to adapt, modify, and alter its structure, functions, and programmes to the needs of a dramatically changing world. I believe that the short sketch of the history of the I.L.O. that I have given in these three lectures suggests that this will certainly be done.

Bibliography

Major Publications on the
International Labor Organization

AMERICAN ACADEMY OF POLITICAL AND SOCIAL SCIENCE. *The International Labor Organisation:* a survey by 21 experts of the work and the relations of one of the three permanent international agencies established under the Treaty of Versailles. Ed. by Alice Cheyney. Philadelphia, 1933. 212 p. (Its: Annals, v. 166, March 1933, pp. 1–207, 235–239)

AYUSAWA, I. F. *History of labor in modern Japan.* Honolulu, East-West Center Press, 1966. xvi, 406 p.

BARNES, G. N. *History of the International Labour Office,* with an introduction by Emile Vandervelde. London, Williams, 1926. 106 p.

BUTLER, H. B. *The lost peace, a personal impression.* London, Faber and Faber, 1941. 224 p.

CHISHOLM, A. *Labour's Magna Charta:* a critical study of the labour clauses of the Peace Treaty and of the draft conventions and recommendations of the Washington International Labour Conference. 2nd ed. London, Green, 1925. xi, 192 p.

FOLLOWS, J. W. *Antecedents of the International Labour Organization.* Oxford, Clarendon Press, 1951. 227 p.

HAAS, E. B. *Beyond the nation state:* functionalism and international organization. Stanford, Stanford University Press, 1964. 595 p.

Bibliography

INTERNATIONAL LABOUR OFFICE. *The International Labour Organisation, the first decade.* Preface by Albert Thomas. London, Allen and Unwin, 1931. 382 p.

JENKS, C. W. *Human rights and international labour standards.* London, Stevens, 1960. xvi, 159 p.

JENKS, C. W. *The international protection of trade union freedom.* London, Stevens, 1957. xi, 592, iv p.

LANDY, E. A. *The effectiveness of international supervision, thirty years of I.L.O. experience.* London, Stevens, 1966. xiii, 268 p.

LORWIN, L. L. *The international labor movement:* history, policies, outlook. New York, Harper, 1953. xviii, 366 p. (Bibliography: pp. 353–357)

MOYNIHAN, D. P. *The U.S. and the I.L.O., 1889–1934.* n.p., 1960. 608 p. (Fletcher School of Law and Diplomacy, thesis) (Microfilm)

PHELAN, E. J. *Albert Thomas et la création du B.I.T.* Paris, Grasset, 1936. 367 p.

PHELAN, E. J. *Yes and Albert Thomas.* London, Cresset Press, 1936. xvi, 270 p.

PILLAI, P. P. *India and the International Labour Organisation.* Patna, Patna University, 1931. 198 p. (Bibliography: pp. 197–198)

PRICE, J. *The international labour movement.* London, Oxford University Press, 1945. x, 273 p. (Royal Institute of International Affairs)

SCELLE, H. *L'Organisation Internationale du Travail et le B.I.T.* Préface d'Albert Thomas. Paris, Rivière, 1930. 349 p.

SHOTWELL, J. T. *The origins of the International Labor Organization.* New York, Columbia University Press, 1934. 2 v.

THOMAS, A. *International social policy.* Geneva, I.L.O., 1948. 162 p.

TROCLET, L. E. *Législation sociale internationale.* Préface de Georges Scelle. Bruxelles, Editions de la Librairie Encyclo-

Bibliography

pédique, 1952. 716 p. (Cahiers de l'Institut de Sociologie Solvay, no. 4.)

WEAVER, G. L. P. *The International Labor Organization and human rights.* [Washington, Howard University, School of Law, 1965.] iii, 54 p.

WILSON, F. G. *The International Labor Organization.* New York, Carnegie Endowment for International Peace, Division of Intercourse and Education, 1932. 63 p. (International conciliation, 284.)

WILSON, F. G. *Labor in the League system:* a study of the International Labor Organization in relation to international administration. Stanford, Stanford University Press, 1934. xii, 384 p. (Bibliography: pp. 365–367)

Index

Acting Director *see* Phelan, Edward

Africa, 38, 39, 42, 47; developing countries of, 43; I.L.O. technical office, 62

African, 44; Advisory Committee, 88; Conference (1960), 61; governments represented on Governing Body, 44; Regional Conference (1970), 88

Agreement(s), among Rhine countries, 67; I.L.O.-U.N., 32

Agriculture, 51, 89, 91; *see also* F.A.O., Labor, agricultural

Amendment(s) *see* Constitution, amendments to

American, Conference at Santiago de Chile, 22, 61; Declaration of Independence, 28; governments represented, 44; professors, 72; regional conferences, 61, 88; *see also* United States

Annuaire de la Société des Nations, 1920–1927, 13n

Apartheid, 41, 42, 108

Area Offices *see* I.L.O. Technical Field Offices

Asia, 38, 47; developing countries of, 43; I.L.O. field office, 62; technical advice, 49; *see also* Developing Countries

Asian, 44; Conference (1947), 61; governments on Governing Body, 44; Regional Conference, 88

Assistant Director *see* Winant, John G.

Australia, 22

Automation, 66, 98

Belgium, 4n; *see also* International Confederation of Free Trade Unions

Berlin, international conference on conditions of labor, 7

Berne, international workers' conference, 7

Bevin, Ernest, 32

Bismarck, Chancellor, 7

Bolivia, 27

Brussels *see* International Confederation of Free Trade Unions

Budget *see* I.L.O.—Financing

Burma, 39

Butler, Harold, 19–21, 23, 23n, 24, 26; *see also* Director-General

Byelorussia, 20n

Canada, 22; Canadian Prime Minister, 26; *see also* Montreal

Ceylon, 39

Chile, 27n, 55; *see also* Santiago de Chile

Christian Trade Union Movement, 44

Collective Bargaining, 10, 29, 32–33, 67, 93, 98

Commission on International Labor Legislation, 4–5, 8, 19

119

Index

Index

45; Evolution of Standard Setting, 56–61; Facing the Gathering Storm (1932–1938), 19–24; 50th Anniversary, 3, 85; financing, 15–16, 27, 33, 37, 47–48, 51; Human Rights, 99–101; Individual Industry Approach, 64–68; national programs, 83; Rationalization and Decentralization, 61–63; Riding the Storm (1939–1943), 24–27; staff, 38; structure and mandate, 8–10; technical field office, 62; The I.L.O. and World Peace, 102–114; The I.L.O. Today, 72–73; The New Outlook (1944–1948), 28–34; World Employment Program, 85–91.

International Labour Review, 12, 27

International Management Institute, 50

International Working Men's Association, 6

Israel, 39, 50

Italy, 4n; government, 70; ratification and veto power, 22; *see also* Genoa, Turin

Japan, 4n, 39; *see also* Tokyo

"Jobs and Skills" Program, 88

Joint Maritime Commission, 64

King, MacKenzie, 26

Labor, administration, 68; agricultural, 12, 15; Labor Charter, 5; forced, 23n; international legislation, 11–12, 19, 32, 94; international standards, 11–12, 17, 27, 33, 45–46, 56–61; 63; labor-management, 18, 29, 51–52, 55, 64, 66, 94; national legislation, 45, 51; problems, 43, 65; *see also* Committees, industrial

Latin America, 22, 27, 47, 47n; I.L.O. field office, 62; Latin Americans, 44; manpower shortages, 49

Leadership, 68–69; *see also* Management Development

League of Nations, 5, 11, 13n, 27, 30; Assembly of, 16; Council of, 22; Italy's veto, 22; relations with I.L.O., 5, 15–16, 21, 30–31

Lebanon, 39

Leeds, international workers' conference, 7

Legislative Series, 12

Legrand (Daniel), 6

Libya, 39

Living Standards, 49, 51, 86, 94, 111; *see also* I.L.O.—Conditions of Work and Life, I.L.O.—The I.L.O. and World Peace, I.L.O.—World Employment Program

London, 26–27, International Labor Office, 13

McNamara, Robert, 110; *see also* World Bank

Management Development, 50, 55, 68, 70–71, 104; *see also* International Center in Turin, Technical Cooperation

Manpower, planning, 88; problems, 33, 49; program, 49; surpluses, 49; *see also* I.L.O.—World Employment Program, Vocational Training

Member States *see* Membership

Membership, 8, 22–23, 39n, 77–78, 113; change in geographical distribution, 43–45; decentralization, 61–62; growth of, 37–38; member states, 88–89, 105, 111; socialism incompatible with, 40; withdrawals, suspension, or expulsion powers, 42; *see also*

Index